M000298199

SEMIOTEXT(E) INTERVENTION SERIES

Published by Semiotext(e)
2007 Wilshire Blvd., Suite 427, Los Angeles, CA 90057
www.semiotexte.com

Thanks to Erik Morse.
The translator wishes to thank Susanna Proietti for her invaluable help.

Design: Hedi El Kholti

ISBN: 978-1-58435-083-5
Distributed by The MIT Press, Cambridge, Mass.
and London, England
Printed in the United States of America

Christian Marazzi

The Violence of

Financial Capitalism

Translated by Kristina Lebedeva

semiotext(e)
intervention
series □ 2

Contents

It's not a question of worrying or of hoping for the best, but of finding new weapons.

— Gilles Deleuze

Introduction

VIOLENT FINANCE

The dancing began in June 2007, when it became known that two hedge funds, managed by Bear Stearns, had invested in assets guaranteed by subprime loans and needed to put $3.8 billion of obligations up for sale. Within one minute, literally, one of the most important investment banks on Wall Street was compelled to sell itself to JP Morgan Chase at defeating prices, $2 per share, when only 48 hours before it cost $30.

A year later, with the bankruptcies of Washington Mutual, Wachovia, Fannie Mae, Freddie Mac, AIG, and Lehman Brothers, and then Citigroup, Bank of America, Northern Rock, UBS, Bank of Scotland, and many other financial institutions, one began to understand that the collapse of Lehman Brothers was not, in fact, an isolated episode and that the entire banking system was in one of the greatest crises of history. Already in December 2007, the central banks of five currency areas announced actions coordinated to sustain the banks. In January 2008, the Central European Bank, the Federal Reserve, and the national Swiss Bank effected additional operations of financing.

Since then there has been an impressive succession of interventions to rescue the banking and financial system, until the last one (March 2009), decided on by the Obama Administration and immediately judged as an nth degree fiasco by the winner of the Nobel prize in economics, Paul Krugman.

The abyss opened by derivative financial products seemed incommensurable. The public deficits increased within a few months to the levels of the Second World War, the geopolitical scenarios were being modified as needed and the crisis, instead of subduing, was inexorably expanding with its most devastating effects on employment, wages, and retirement. On the bare life of entire populations.

It is the crisis of crises, a crisis that has a long story and, in all likelihood, a long future. It is a violent crisis, of a violent finance, a crisis that witnessed the greats of the world economy (G20) meeting in London, April 2, concerned with reviving the global economy by actions of intervention that only partially reflected the gravity of the problems accumulated through years of financialization of economy. It is a systemic crisis that saw an entire economic, political, and cultural model collapse under the pressure of its own contradictions, a crisis in which anger, disenchantment, distrust, and protest are limited to questioning the very limits of capitalism.

1

THE BECOMING OF THE CRISIS

Before interpreting the crisis of financial capitalism, it may be useful to summarize some facts about the macro-economic and global financial situation that has been emerging for more than a year, as a result of the real estate and banking bubble. Let us say from the outset, citing an article by Martin Wolf, an intelligent supporter of liberal globalization in the *Financial Times* (January 7, 2009), that, although necessary, the dramatic increase of the American federal deficit and the expansion of credit from central banks all over the world will have *temporary effects* but will not be able to restore normal and lasting rates of development. It is thus possible that over the course of 2009, and beyond, we will witness the succession of a false recovery, a hiccups movement in the stock exchange followed by repetitive downfalls and subsequent interventions of governments attempting to contain the crisis. In short, we are confronted by a systemic crisis requiring "radical changes" that, at least for the time being, no one can really prescribe in a convincing manner. The monetary policy, even if it has some efficacy in improving economies during recessions, is entirely ineffective when it enters into a depressive crisis like the one we are living in. The reason is that in a crisis like the present one (*The Economist* called it "the biggest bubble in history"), which in some sense resembles what Japan experienced in the 1990s, the transmission channels of monetary interventions (reduction of interest rate, insertion of liquidity, interventions in the exchange rate, increase in the banking reserve funds) are beside the point. That is, they cannot transmit the credit impulses to companies and domestic economies necessary to revive the consumption. The difference being that, in the case of Japan, the bubble burst had depressive effects on investments in capital, which up until the 1980s represented 17% of Gross Domestic Product, while the crisis that broke out in the United States had direct effects on 70% of GDP resulting from the consumption in the domestic American economies. Given that "the US consumer is by far the most important consumer in the world, the global implications of America's post-bubble shake-out are likely to be far more severe than those Japan was subjected to" (Stephen Roach, "US Not Certain of Avoiding Japan-Style 'Lost Decade,'" *Financial Times*, January 14, 2009).

On the basis of a study by Carmen Reinhart from Maryland University and Kenneth Rogoff from Harvard ("The Aftermath of Financial Crises," December 2008, http://www.economics.harvard.edu/

faculty/rogofff/files/Aftermath.pdf), we see in what way this crisis is by far the deepest in the past few decades. Banking crises like this one, as the authors note in retrospect, last at least two years with severe drops in GDP. The collapses in the stock markets are profound, with an average fall in real prices of real estate assets equaling 35% over the span of 6 years and a 55% decline in prices of non-real estate assets over 3–4 years. The unemployment rate, always averaged, rose by 7% in 4 years, while the output decreased by 9%. Moreover, the real value of public debt increased, on average, by 86% and this is only in small part due to the cost of bank recapitalization. Instead, it largely depends on the collapse of tax revenues.

An important difference between this crisis and the ones in the recent past is that the present one is a *global* crisis and not regional, like the others. Until, like in the past, the rest of the world is in the position of being able to finance the US, we can anticipate a containment of the crisis on a regional scale. This is because to the extent that the American government can take advantage of a vast program of tax and monetary stimuli financed by the countries in surplus of saving from the purchase of American Treasury bills. But who today can help the US in the long run? The present difficulty consists in the fact that, being global, the crisis broke the very force that allowed the global economy to grow, albeit in an unequal way, over the last decades, i.e., the flux of demand from the countries in the structural deficit of production (like the US) to the countries in structural surplus (like China, Japan, Germany). But when private spending collapses on a global scale, the efforts to increase the American demand no longer suffice. That is to say, actions to revive the demand on a global scale will be required, even in the emerging countries with a surplus of production. At the moment, it does not seem that the emerging countries can compensate for the loss of demand internal to the developed countries (so-called *decoupling*), since for them the crisis has particularly heavy depressive effects as well. Nonetheless, according to the estimate of the World Bank, it cannot be excluded that, at least in the medium range (2010–2015) and with important differences between China, India, Russia, and South American countries, the growth rates will continue to be maintained at an average of 4–5%. This possibility depends on the fact that of the total of exports in the emerging countries (which averaged 35% of GDP in the emerging countries over the last 5 years) only 20% are exports to the developed countries, while 15% results from internal exchanges between the block of the emerging countries ("Emerging Markets: Stumble or Fall?" *The Economist*, January 10, 2009). In any case, in order to be able to pull the world demand, the emerging countries must—besides raising internal wages—channel their savings no longer towards the Western countries in deficit, but towards internal demand, which robs the global monetary and financial circuit of the same mechanism that allowed the global economy to function despite, even because of profound structural imbalances. It is thus possible that, *after the crisis*, the emerging countries will become the hegemonic economic force in which the savings of the developed countries will be invested, thereby inverting flows of capital and somewhat reducing the level of consumption in the developed countries. But no one can foresee the *duration* of this crisis and, therefore, the political, in addition to economic, capacity to manage the cumulative multiplication of social and political contradictions that are already manifesting themselves.

Thus, the least we can do is focus our attention on the trend of demand in the advanced deficit countries, particularly in the US. If we take into account that, in the US, between the third quarter of 2007 and the third quarter of 2008, the fall of demand in private credit equaled 13%, it is certain that the net saving is destined to remain positive for several years—and not just in the US. In other words, private citizens will do everything to reduce their private debts, which can only annul the monetary actions for the revival of private consumption. Assuming for a moment a financial surplus (that is, lack of consumption) in the private sector of 6% of GDP and a structural deficit in the commercial balance of 4% of GDP, the tax deficit necessary to compensate for the reduction of internal and external demand would have to be, according to Wolf's estimate in the cited article, equal to 10% of GDP—"*indefinitely*"! Reducing public debts of such a scale entails enormous efforts, especially if we take into account that already today the federal American deficit moves around 12% of GDP—at the levels of the Second World War.

As if this were not enough, we should not forget that the obstacles to debt redemption for companies caused by nominal interest rates tending to zero and the reduction of prices (deflation): in situations of this kind, real interest rates are very high and debt repayment consequently becomes very challenging. It is precisely for this reason that a second wave of banking crises cannot be excluded. As Michael Aglietta writes, "If such is the situation, the banks are risking a second financial shock—return shock, one of the insolvent credits of companies. It is thus that an economic depression can propagate itself by reciprocal reinforcement of debt redemption in finance and economic deflation" (*La crise. Pourquoi en est-on arrivé là? Comment en sortir?*, Michalon, Parigi, 2008, p. 118).

According to Paul Krugman, the $825 billion of the economic stimulus program proposed by

Obama (then reduced by Congress and the Senate, on February 11, to $789.5 billion) is not even remotely sufficient to fill the "productivity gap" between the potential growth and effective growth of GDP at the time of the crisis: "In the presence of an adequate demand for productive capacity, in the next two years America would be able to produce goods and services worth another thirty trillion. But with the downturn of consumption and investment, an enormous chasm is opening up between that which the American economy can produce and that which it can sell. And Obama's plan is not minimally adequate to fill in this productivity gap." Now, Krugman wonders, why is Obama not trying to do more? Certainly, there are dangers tied up with the government loan on the vast scale, "but the consequences of inadequate action are not much better than sliding into a prolonged deflationary trap, of the Japanese kind," an inevitable spiral if the actions of intervention are not adequate (i.e., around $2.1 billion or trillion). Or, Krugman keeps wondering, is it the lack of spending opportunities that limits his plan? "There are only a limited number of shovel-ready projects for public investment, that is, of projects which can be initiated rapidly enough to succeed in the short-term boost of economy. Nonetheless, there are other forms of public spending, especially in the field of health care, which can create assets and at the same time foster the economy at the time of need." Yet again, is there an element of political prudence behind Obama's decision, i.e., the attempt to remain within the limit of a trillion dollars for the economic plan's final cost to ensure the support of the Republicans? ("Il piano Obama non basta," *La Reppublica*, January 10, 2009).

Obama's plan is composed of 60% public spending (health care, investments in infrastructure and education, aids to homeowners risking foreclosure) and 35% tax reductions. Joseph Stiglitz, in his interview in the *Financial Times* ("Do not Squander America's Stimulus on Tax Cut," 16 January, 2009) has, however, urged not to squander the stimulus on tax breaks, which, in this crisis, are doomed for a sure failure. For example, only 50% of the tax cut that came into effect in February 2008 increased spending, while the remaining part of the increase in available income was used to reduce private debts. Today a tax break would most likely be used almost completely to reduce the debts, except perhaps in the case of poor families with a high tendency to consumption. It would be much better, if one indeed wants to persist on the path of tax cuts, to limit the breaks of all companies to increases in investments, preferably if they are innovative. "Spending on infrastructure, education and technology create assets; they increase future productivity" (Stiglitz).

Independently of the fact that the state stimuli result mainly from increases in discretionary expenditures, like in the US, or by the more or less automatic effects of an increase in social spending, like in Europe, the state governance of the crisis depends in the last analysis on the capacity to borrow capital from the bond market. The dimension of the issuance of public bonds scheduled for 2009 is sky-high: it goes from the estimated 2, maybe $2.5 billion in the US, equaling 14% of GDP, to $215 billion worth of bonds sold in England (10% of GDP), to issuances of significant amounts of bonds in every country of the world, including Germany, which at first, tried to resist tax stimuli of the Anglo-Saxon kind (initially accused of "crass Keynesianism" by chancellor Merkel).

The recourse to the bond markets on the part of the US in order to collect capital to cover the growing deficit should not, in principle, be a particular problem, especially in deflationary periods, like the one we are going through, characterized by continuous reductions in interest rates (which for investors in bonds means real fixed and relatively high earnings).

Nonetheless, the expectation of a recurrence of inflation, caused by the strong increases in deficit and public debt and by massive injections of currency, and, consequently, of a loss of earning from the State's bonds, is already provoking an increase in real interest rates on T-bills, and this is also the case in the economically wealthiest countries. In fact, international investors in public bonds demand substantially higher nominal and real earnings in order to better protect themselves against the risks of state defaults. According to the analysts, as much as there are signals of an economic bubble on the markets that can explain the distortion of prices, "it is nonetheless somewhat unsettling that real interest rates have risen as governments started to borrow" (Chris Giles, David Oakley, and Michael Mackenzie, "Onerous issuance," *Financial Times*, January 7, 2009; see also Steve Johnson, "Inflation Fears to Hit Debt Auction," *FT Weekly Review of the Fund Management Industry*, March 30, 2009). For countries like Spain, Portugal, Greece, Ireland, and Italy, whose differential earnings in T-bills had been been a little higher than those of Germany until 2007, the problems with financing public deficits have been increasing in an obvious way since December 2008.

Alfonso Tuor has summarized the consequences of the crisis of the public debt on a world scale as follows: "the short-term consequence of these policies is a crisis of trust in bonds with which the States finance the public debt. There is no lack of premonitory signals: the last in the order of time came from Great Britain, where, for the first time over the last seven years an auction of public bonds failed, despite the decision of the Bank of England to purchase them for more than 100 billion euros. The crisis of the public debt is destined to provoke a subsequent escalation of interventions in the central banks. The latter would be called upon to buy them in large quantities and to print more currency. With what consequences? A strong inflation, if there is the interlude of a short recovery, or, in some countries (the top candidates are Great Britain and the US), currency crises and hyperinflation. Which, for the citizen, means an impressive destruction of private and retirement savings, but for the financial oligarchy an ideal instrument to destroy the value of the enormous quantity of toxic activities held by the large banks" ("Chi pagherà il conto della crisi?," Corriere del Ticino, March 27, 2009).

Despite the ten years of the euro, the markets are working with precise distinctions between the risk countries within this very eurozone—a problem not easily resolvable by the recourse to the creation of a currency by the United Nations or by releasing unionbonds, which would damage the strong countries in the eurozone. This again urgently raises the question of a real unification of state policies, particularly the social ones, within the UN.

In this phase, with few investors disposed to purchase public obligations in the face of an extremely high offer to issue public bonds, the risk of crowding out (of leaving the private bond market) is entirely real. The competition in bond markets between private companies and governments risks further inhibiting the overcoming of the crisis, to the extent that, for the companies involved, the issuance of bonds can become particularly costly. At this point, the State—as it is already happening in the US with the support of the car companies—can be compelled to support private companies directly by purchasing their bonds, which would mean the beginning of a process of quasi-nationalization (without, however, the right to vote from the stockholder State) of non-financial companies. This process would follow the one that began in the banking and financial sector with the interventions of central banks in the last months. If then, as a hypothesis, the world economy were to start up again, the process inverse of crowding out, i.e., the withdrawal of public bonds towards the private ones, would significantly increase debt service in all the indebted countries.

"The hopes of overcoming the crisis," writes Alfonso Tuor, "are melting like the snow under the sun. A series of negative news are curbing even the most incurable optimists and forcing stock to go down to levels less than the lowest registered in the course of November" ("Crisi dell'Est, nuovo incubo dell'Europa," *Corriere del Ticino*, February 19, 2009). The crisis of the former Soviet bloc countries, which in the last years have been indebted to the European banks in Swiss francs, American dollars, Japanese yen, Swedish crowns, and euro—in order to compensate for the scarcity of internal savings and to reinforce the expansion of credit to small and medium companies, the expansion of mortgage credit to low interest rates and real estate overinvestments—seriously risks boomeranging against the European banks. The latter, particularly the Austrian, Italian, and Swedish banks, have acquired significant shareholding (up to 80%) in Hungarian, Slovenian, and Slovak banks, which means that an insolvency crisis in the domestic East European economies—a crisis entirely similar to those of Mexico, Argentina, or Southeast Asia, a kind of European subprime crisis—immediately becomes a problem of the European Union, in addition to that of its banks. "The crisis started in the US, but Europe is where it might turn into catastrophe," writes Wolfgang Münchau ("Eastern Crisis That Could Wreck the Eurozone," *Financial Times*, February 23, 2009). In this case, actions of intervention to support Eastern economies, as, for example, an intervention of the International Monetary Fund, to escape a contagious crisis of payment balances due to a chain of devaluations of local currencies, seem entirely inefficient. "If the exchange rates," wonders Münchau, "were to go down even more, the failures of domestic economies could increase dramatically. Are we, Europeans, ready to help them?" It is difficult to imagine European citizens running to help the mythic Polish plumber. The split at the heart of

Europe due to the collapse of the former communist Soviet bloc seriously risks calling into question the very future of the EU ("The Bill That Could Break up Europe," *The Economist*, February 28, 2009).

The scenario at the forefront here is a massive and continuous increase in unemployment on a world scale, and a generalized reduction in incomes and rent [rendita], in the face of a vertiginous increase in a comprehensive tax deficit. The financial crisis has had its devastating effects on the manufacturing industry and its world commerce, with millions of dismissals, closedowns of thousands of factories, biblical returns of immigrants to their countries of origin ("The Collapse of Manufacturing," *The Economist*, February 21, 2009). For the moment, that is, beginning from the crises of the Bear Stearns, proceeding to the crisis of the Lehman Brothers, American International Group, and of Citigroup, the "socialist turn" of liberal governments to sustain the banking, financial, and insurance system by means of recapitalization and monetary issuances does not seem to be able to avoid chain bankruptcy of all insolvent decentralized banks due to an improbable quantity of toxic assets. "It would take another $1.5 billion," writes the economist Nouriel Roubini from New York University, "to restore the capital of banks to the pre-crisis level: only thus will it be possible to overcome the credit constraint and revive loans to the private sectors. In other words, the US banking system is in fact insolvent on the whole, just like the large part of the British banking system and many banks in continental Europe" ("La voragine dei conti USA," *La Repubblica*, February 26, 2009). There is no sufficient private capital to absorb the present and foreseeable losses and reconstruct bank assets. The resources for this must be public (whether one likes it or not). The slowness in recognizing that it is a question, no more and no less, of an insolvency crisis of the banking system as a whole, will involve extremely high prices. The same is true for the difficulty undoing the knot, certainly complex, of the nationalization of the major banks (even on the day when the American State becomes the principal shareholder of the colossal Citigroup with 36% of capital stock).

It is entirely likely that in two years the economies of all countries, despite the actions of the economic stimulus, will still be in depression (stag deflation), just as it is possible that each country will try to reintroduce in their native land the quotas of demand by means of devaluations and protectionist actions (deglobalization) in order to try to postpone as much as possible the rendering of accounts by taxpayers called on to pay public deficits. The margins of economic and monetary policy to effectively manage the crisis are extremely restricted. The classical Keynesian actions lack transmission channels of state stimuli to the real economy, to the demand of goods and services, and investment goods. On the other hand, it makes little sense to speak of a new Bretton Woods without taking into account the profound transformations in the international monetary arrangement, the transformations that reflect the crisis of national sovereignty resulting from globalization. If one instead wants to speak of a New Deal, i.e., of a process of supporting incomes, employment, and credit system at the "grassroots" level, it will then be necessary to analyze social forces, subjects, and forms of struggle that can substantiate in a politically innovative way the escape from the crisis.

2

FINANCIAL LOGICS

The process of financialization that led to the crisis we are living in now is distinguished from all other phases of financialization historically recorded in the twentieth century. The classical financial crises were situated at a precise moment of the economic cycle, particularly at the end of the cycle, in conjunction with a fall of profit testing as a result of capitalist competition on an international scale, in addition to social forces undermining geopolitical equilibrium in the international division of labor. The typical twentieth-century financialization thus represented an attempt, in certain ways "parasitic" and "desperate," to recuperate on the financial markets that which capital could no longer get in the real economy. As Charles P. Kindleberger, the greatest historian of finance, showed, since the 17th century financial cycles have always consisted of a precise sequence: a phase of impetus, one of collective infatuation and overtrading of stock markets, a phase of fear and disorder, then a phase of consolidation, and, finally, a phase of reorganization. "In the phase of overtrading (*emballement*), activity becomes frenetic, the aspirations of individuals do not cease to grow, the velocity of transactions is accelerated, and the prices of real or virtual financial assets—that is, the price of elements constitutive of people's wealth—are inflamed" (M. Aglietta, *op. cit.*, p. 8). The accumulation and specific centralization of the "capital bearer of interest," as Marx defined it in Volume III of *Capital*, also called "fictitious capital," managed primarily by banks with autonomous production of money by means of money indeed epitomized one of the salient characteristics of the twentieth century financialization processes (and pointed out by Marx over the course of the second half of the nineteenth century). The financial crises were thus based on a contradictory relationship between real and financial economies, a relationship that today is no longer expressed in the same terms.

The financial economy today is pervasive, that is, it spreads across the entire economic cycle, co-existing with it, so to speak, from start to finish. Today it is in the finances, to speak figuratively, even when one goes shopping at the supermarket, at the moment when one pays with a credit card. The car industry, to give only one example, functions completely in accordance with credit mechanisms (installments, leasing, etc.), so that the problems of a General Motors have just as much to do with the production of cars as, if not above all, with the weakness of GMAC, its branch specializing in credit to consumption indispensable for selling their products to consumers.

That is, we are in a historical period in which the finances are *cosubstantial* to the very production of goods and services.

In addition to industrial profits not reinvested in instrumental capitals and in wages, the sources fueling today's financialization have multiplied: there are profits deriving from the repatriation of dividends and royalties followed by direct investments from the outside; flows of interest coming from the Third World's debt, to which are added flows of interest on international bank loans to the emerging countries; surplus-values derived from raw materials; the sums accumulated by individuals and wealthy families and invested in the stock markets, retirement and investment funds. The multiplication and extension of the sources and agents of the "capital bearer of interest" are, without a doubt, one of the distinctive, unforeseen, and problematic traits of the new financial capitalism, especially if they reflect upon the possibility or impossibility of modifying this system, of "re-financing" it, reestablishing a "more balanced" relation between the real and financial economies.

Like its predecessors, this financialization also begins from a block of accumulation understood as non-reinvestment of profits in directly productive processes (constant capital, i.e., instrumental goods, and variable capital, i.e., wages). In fact, it began with the crisis of growth of Fordist capitalism since the 1960s. In those years, there were all the premises of a repetition of classical financialization based on the dichotomy between real (industrial) and monetary economies, with the consequent seizing of profit quotas on the financial markets to ensure profitable growth without accumulation. In the beginning of the 1980s, "the primary source of financial bubbles was the trend of growth of non-accumulated profit, the growth caused by a double movement: on the one hand, a generalized decrease in wages and, on the other hand, the stagnation—i.e., decrease—of the rate of accumulation despite the reestablishment of profit rate" (Michel Husson, "Les enjeux de la crise," *La Brèche*, November 2008). For an accumulation rate implies the growth of the amount of net capital, while profit rate implies the relationship between profits and capital: the divergence between the two rates starting from 1980 represents a sure indication of financialization. But, as we said, to the non-reinvested industrial profits are gradually added other sources of "accumulation" of financial capital, a fact to keep in mind in order to understand the transformations of the model of post-Fordist crisis-development. In particular, financialization involved a process of banking de-mediation regarding the financialization of economic growth (the pre-dominance of the Anglo-Saxon model over the Rhenish one), but also involved a process of the *multiplication* of financial intermediaries resulting from the deregulation and liberation of economy.

The transition from the Fordist mode of production to "stock managerial capitalism," which is at the basis of today's financial capitalism, is, in fact, explained by the drop in profits (around 50%) between the 1960s and the 1970s; the drop due to the exhaustion of the technological and economic foundations of Fordism, particularly by the saturation of markets by mass consumption goods, the rigidity of productive processes, of constant capital, and of the politically "downwardly rigid" [*rigido verso il basso*] working wage. At the height of its development, in a determinate organic composition of capital (i.e., the relationship between constant and variable capital), Fordist capitalism was no longer able to "suck" surplus-value from living working labor. "Hence, since the second half of the 1970s, the primary propulsive force of the world economy was the endless attempt of capitalist companies—demanded by their owners and investors—to bring back by different means the profit rate to the highest levels of twenty years ago" (Luciano Gallino, *L'impresa irresponsabile*, Einaudi, Torino, 2005). We know how it went: reduction in the cost of labor, attacks on syndicates, automatization and robotization of entire labor processes, delocalization in countries with low wages, precarization of work, and diversification of consumption models. And precisely financialization, i.e., increase in profits not as excess of cost proceeds (that is, not in accordance with manufacturing-Fordist logic) but as excess of value in the

Stock Exchange "at the time T2 with respect to T1—where the gap between T1 and T2 can be a few days."

In fact, the recourse to the financial markets on the part of companies in order to reestablish profit testing has really never had anything to do with financing company activities by issuing new bonds—and this is because companies have always had wide margins of self-financing. American companies, the companies in the largest shareholding country in the world, have used financing by the issuances of assets to supply only 1% of their needs; the German companies 2%. In other words, the financialization of economy has been a process of recuperation of capital's profitability after the period of decrease in profit testing, an apparatus to enhance capital's profitability *outside* immediately productive processes. It is this very apparatus that led companies to internalize in an "irresponsible" way the paradigm of shareholder value, the primacy of shareholder value over that of the multiplicity of "interest bearers"—the latter being called stakeholder value (wage earners, consumers, suppliers, environment, future generations). The (industrial) profit quota of the total income of companies, which in the 1960s and 1970s decreased in the US from 24% to 15–17%, has never since exceeded 14–15%, and financialization is structured accordingly, becoming for all intents and purposes the modus operandi of contemporary capitalism.

"As was shown on the basis of Greta Krippner's complete analysis of available data, the quota of total profits of American companies attributable to the financial, insurance, and real estate companies not only nearly reached in the 1980s, but then exceeded in the 1990s, the quota attributable to those in the manufacturing sector. Even more important is the fact that, in the 1970s and 1980s, the non-financial companies would drastically increased their own investments in financial products with respect to industrial plants and machinery and became ever more dependent on the quota of income and profits derived from their own financial investments with respect to the one derived from their productive activity. Krippner's observation is that, within this tendency towards the financialization of the non-financial economy, the manufacturing sector is not only quantitatively predominant, but directly driving the process, is particularly significant" (Giovanni Arrighi, *Adam Smith a Pechino. Genealogie del ventunesimo secolo*, Feltrinelli, Milano, 2007, pp. 159–160). This is enough to definitively discard the distinction between (industrial) real and financial economies, distinguishing industrial profits from the "fictitious" financial ones. As well as to stop identifying, from either a theoretical or historical point of view, capitalism with industrial capitalism (as Arrighi writes, a typical act of faith of orthodox Marxism that does not deserve the justification). If one really wants to speak of the "irresponsible company" to describe the paradigm of shareholder value—indeed created within companies over the last thirty years—one would do well to speak of the transformation of the production process based on the "profits becoming rent," to use Carlo Vercellone's apt expression ("Crisi della legge del valore e divenire rendita dei profitti," in *Crisi dell'economia globale. Mercati finanziari, lotte sociali e nuovi scenari politici*, ed. by Andrea Fumagali and Sandro Mezzandra, Ombre Corte/*Uni*nomade, Verona, 2009).

There is no doubt that, in the post-Fordist configuration of financial capitalism, where part of the wages are reduced and precarized and investments in capital stagnate, the problem of the *realization* of profits (that is, selling the surplus-value product) remains the role of consumption by means of *non-wage incomes*. Under this *distributive* profile, the reproduction of capital (characterized by the extremely high polarization of wealth) is carried out partly thanks to the increase in the consumption of rentiers and partly thanks to the indebted consumption of wage earners. Financialization has redistributed, although in a strongly unequal and precarious way (if one thinks of retirement incomes derived from supplementary retirement funds in accordance with the primacy of contributions), financial incomes to wage workers in the double form of non-real-estate and real estate incomes (in the US, 20% and 89% respectively). There is thus a kind of becoming-rent in addition to profit.

The indebtedness of domestic economies, to which corresponds a more or less pronounced reduction of savings according to whether one is in the US or

Europe, is what allowed financial capitalism to reproduce itself on an enlarged and global scale. It is possible to affirm that, parallel to the reduction of the redistributive function of the social State, in this period it is assisted by a kind of privatization of deficit spending à la Keynes, i.e., the creation of an additional demand by means of private debt (with a relative displacement of wealth towards the private domestic economies).

The American mortgage indebtedness, which reached more than 70% of GDP with a total indebtedness of domestic economies equaling 93% of GDP, has constituted the primary source of increase in consumption since 2000 and, since 2002, the motor of the real estate bubble. The consumption has been fueled by so-called remortgaging, the possibility of renegotiating mortgage loans in order to get new credit, thanks to the inflationary increase in house prices. This mechanism, called home equity extraction, has played a fundamental role in the American economic growth. The US Bureau of Economic Analysis has estimated that the gains from the GDP growth due to the increase in home equity extraction were, on average, 1.5% between 2002 and 2007. Without the positive impact of mortgage credit and the subsequent increase in consumption, the growth of American GDP would be equal to, or outright less than, that of the eurozone (Jacques Sapir, *L'économie politique internationale de la crise et la question du "nouveau Bretton Woods": Leçons pour des temps de crise, Mimeo*, sapir@msh-paris.fr).

The explosion of private indebtedness was facilitated, especially after the collapse of Nasdaq in 2000–2002, by a very expansive monetary policy and banking deregulation, a policy that reinforced the securitization of debt-based obligations: Collaterized Debt Obligation and Collaterized Loan Obligations, to which are added Credit Default Swaps, derivative insurance obligations that are swapped (in fact, bartered) between operators in order to protect themselves against the risks of investment. The total of all these credit derivatives amounts to something like $62 trillion, a multiplication of 100 in ten years (for a description of securitized bonds and other financial instruments, see the brief dictionary in the Appendix).

Securitization allows one to reclaim from the balances of institutions or credit agencies (mortgage, but also credit card) the loans supplied by clients selling them to investment banks. The latter constitutes a credit pool with differentiated risks (from good to less good) and, on this basis, issue assets, which are then ceded to the created *ad hoc* financial structures (called conduits and special vehicles) that finance the purchase price by short-term debts. Finally, bonds are placed with investors as hedge funds, investment banks, retirement and investment funds. In such a way, someone's mortgage debts become a high-paying business (as long as it lasts) in the hands of someone else.

"In order to describe this mechanism, we use the expression *originate-to-distribute*. As in a production chain, various specialized firms coordinate their shares in order to fabricate, assemble, and synthesize investment products beginning from aggregates of real estate credits. The actors in this chain are brokers of real estate loans, directly in contact with consumers, the intermediaries who buy wholesale and bring together credit aggregates in accordance with the specifications of financial institutions and hedge funds (that, in the end of the chain, provide capital), and, finally, rating agencies that determine whether the composition of these asset portfolios satisfies their criteria of quality" (Martha Poon, "Aux origines était la bulle. La mécanique des fluides des subprimes," http://www.mouvements.info/spip.php?article379).

This complex financial engineering, in its good nature, allows for the artificial increase of the total amount of credit (leverage effect), freeing the balances of the institutions from credit given in this way in order to enable them to create new loans. It is a question of multiplication of bread because a split between flows of bonds *qua* right to a part of created profit and flows of purely monetary interests and dividends is inherent in the multiplication of credit by means of securitization.

There is no doubt that derivative obligations created on subprime mortgage credits immediately became the scapegoat of the financial world crisis so much as to obtain the name of "toxic" assets. The securitization of subprime loans is, in fact, situated at the center of the transformations of the world of American mortgage finance where the industry of real estate loans is articulated by the vastest market of investment products based on activities (asset-backed securities). In the latter are condensed all the evils of the new finance: laxist practices of credit, rushing to search for easy compensating money from the issued bonds on loans, the confidence in the supplying of loans to financially untrustworthy people, the violation of rules, the naiveté in calculating risks, frauds, etc.

As Martha Poon reminds us in the article we just cited, "the system of exchanging real estate credits is not a novelty in the US, since it goes back to the New Deal. But in the recent period, there has been a sliding of this traditionally circumscribed practice to a market whose liquidity was sustained by organisms guaranteed by the State—the governments-sponsored enterprises or GSE, usually called Freddie Mac and Fannie Mae—and by specialized lenders whose activity was financed by deposits in the management largely pulled by investments in risk-capital." It is also true that in the GSE the only securitized loans were the prime ones, while the subprime loans were by definition excluded (on the creation, in 1971, of the prime derivative obligation, called "Ginnie Mae," let me refer to my book *E il denaro va. Esodo e revoluzione dei mercati finanziari*, Bollati Boringhieri/Edizioni Casagrande, Torino-Bellinzona, 1998, pp. 65–69).

"The financial crisis," writes Paul Krugman, "inevitably unleashed the hunt for the culprits. Some charges were totally false, such as the thesis, popular on the right, according to which all our problems are caused by the Community Reinvestment Act, which obligates the banks to give out loans to the members of minorities who wish to buy a house and who then cannot repay the loans. In reality, this law was approved in 1977, making it hard to understand how it could be guilty of a crisis determined three decades later. In any case, the Community Reinvestment Act applied only to the deposit banks which had a minimal quota in the real estate bubble" (*Il ritorno dell'economia della depressione e de la crisi del 2008*, Garzanti, Milano, 2009, pp. 182–183).

Moreover, it may be useful to recall that the securitization of prime loans in the course of the 1970s and 1980s has facilitated the expansion of not only the American middle class. "During the years of inflation, the Americans, Canadians, Japanese, and the large part of Europe underwent the fascination with owning a house. The price on houses was going up until it had no relationship with the purchase price, and everyone was satisfied. Satisfied at least while the abundance lasted, especially since the ownership cost quite a lot. The inflation of the value of houses was in fact a powerful mechanism of redistributing wealth. Whoever did not have his own house was at a disadvantage: like everyone, he continued to pay for evermore expensive goods and services, but, in contrast to owners, was not compensated by gains in capital account exempt from levies" (Marco d'Eramo, *Il maiale e il grattacielo. Chicago: una storia del nostro futuro*, Feltrinelli, Milano, 1995, p. 39).

Beginning with the 2000–2002 crisis of the new economy, the American real estate market witnessed a spectacular acceleration, especially if we recall that, already in 2001, the real estate prices were considerably high; so high that the analysts were considering there would be a bubble in the sector in 2002. Instead, thanks to the securitization of subprime loans, it was possible to postpone the inflation of the real estate sector until the bubble burst in 2007.

The expansion of subprime loans shows that, in order to raise and make profits, finance needs to involve the poor, in addition to the middle class. In order to function, this capitalism must invest in the bare life of people who cannot provide any guarantee, who offer nothing apart from themselves. It is a capitalism that turns bare life into a direct source of profit. It does so on the basis of a probability calculation according to which the lacking debt repayment is considered "manageable," i.e., negligible, when considered on the scale of the entire population. The financial logic underlying the calculation of probability is, in fact, particularly cynical: the assets issued on the basis of the mortgage credit pool and grouped together by investment banks are created in accordance with the principle of subordination, i.e., a hierarchy of risks internal to the issued assets. The first lot, the lesser one, would have a high risk. The intermediate one would present a reduced risk, and the highest one, made up of oldest, best assets, would be considered particularly secure. The greater lot is thus *protected* by the lesser ones, in the sense that the latter will be the most exposed part of the securitized assets that will be the first to explode. The access to a good house is created on the basis of mathematical models of risk where people's life means absolutely nothing, where the poor are "played" against the less poor, where the social right to housing is artificially subordinated to the private right to realize a profit. No offence to the academic economists who all these years have been putting their scientific competence and their dignity at the disposal of financial industry (on how today's financial crisis also reveals the crisis of academic economic science, see David Colander et al., "The Financial Crisis and the Systemic Failure of Academic Economics," http://economistsview.typepad.com/eco nomistsview/2009/02/the-financial-crisis-and-the-sys temic-failure-of-academic-economics.html).

Finance functions on the expectation of growing and "infinite" increases in prices of real estate (wealth effect), an inflationary increase without which it would be impossible to co-opt the potential have-nots—the necessary condition of ensuring the continuity of financial profits. It is a question of a Ponzi scheme or an airplane game in which those who came in last allow those who came in first to be renumbered. This is something the hoax devised by the ex-president of

Nasdaq, Bernard Madoff, teaches us, the hoax that managed to collect something like $50 billion involving an impressive number of respectable financial operators and banks.

The threshold of this inclusive process is given in the contradiction between social ownership of a good (such as the house) and private ownership rights, between the expansion of social needs and the private logic of markets. The social conflict as well as capital's capacity or incapacity to overcome this crisis unfolds on this threshold. It is a question of a *temporal threshold*, if only one thinks of, for example, the architecture of typical mortgage contracts on subprime loans. The formula of 2 + 28—where, in the first two years, mortgage interests are fixed and low, precisely for co-opting evermore "owners," and the other 28 years they are at variable rates, thus subjected to the general trend of conjuncture and of monetary policy—represents an example of the contradiction between social ownership rights and private property rights. After two years of relative governance of use-value (the right to the access to housing), we move on to 28 years of governance of exchange-value, with extremely violent effects of expulsion/exclusion. In such a way, the financial logic produces a *commune* (of goods) [*un (bene) comune*] that then divides and privatizes through expelling "residents of the commune" by means of the artificial creation of *scarcity* of all kinds— scarcity of financial means, liquidity, rights, desire, and power. This is a process that reminds us of the time of the seventeenth century enclosures where the peasants—living on and off the land as a common good—were expunged by the processes of privatization and division of the common land, the processes that gave rise to the modern proletariat and its bare life.

When Augusto Illuminati speaks of Spinoza and his resistance to the norm and the discipline of sovereignty, he highlights the decidedly juridical-normative nature of the processes of enclosures: Spinoza "does not ignore the land, but his campaign is not circumscribed by the eighteenth century enclosures, fenced in by farming and hunting, where the sheep—to speak with the *Levellers*—devoured men. It is not circumscribed by the land where men are reduced to inert sheep learning only to serve, because it is neither peace nor citizenship, but rather *solitude*, desert" (*Spinoza atlantico*, Edizioni Ghilbi, Milano, 2008, p. 15). The originary or primitive accumulation, as was shown by Sandro Mezzandra, i.e., the salarization and proletarization of millions of people through the expulsion from their own land, is thus a process that historically reemerges every time the expansion of capital clashes with the commune produced by social relations and cooperations free from the laws of capitalist exploitation (S. Mezzadra, *La "cosiddetta" accumulazione originaria*, in AAVV, Lessico marxiano, minifestolibri, Roma, 2008). The commune produced by free social relations thus *precedes* the capitalist appropriation of this very commune.

3

ON THE RENT BECOMING PROFIT

The *non*-parasitic role of finance, its capacity to produce incomes by ensuring the increase in consumption, the increase in effective demand necessary for GDP growth, is, however, not explained only from the distributive point of view. It is indeed true that finance nourishes itself on the profit that is not accumulated, not reinvested in capital (constant and variable), and it is exponentially multiplied thanks to financial engineering, just as it is true that the increase in profits allows for the distribution of surplus-value quotas to the holders of patrimonial shares. Under this profile (*distributive*, let us repeat), the analysis of financialization and its intrinsic instability highlights real and indeed perverse processes of autonomization of financial capital from any collective interest (wage and occupational stability, the collapse of retirement rents and of savings invested in stock, the impossibility of accessing consumption in credit, the vaporization of stocks in research). It highlights dynamic auto-referentials where the search for ever-higher share-holder earnings generates the increase of fictitious profits by the proliferation of financial instruments—unmanageable because they are outside every rule and control.

The crisis-development in this mode of production acquires a discrepancy between social needs and financial logics based on the hyper-profitability criteria: in the developed countries, it is asserted by the anthropogenic model of "production of man by man" where consumption is increasingly oriented towards social, health, educational, and cultural sectors, and clashes with the privatization of many sectors previously managed by public criteria; in the emerging countries, the expansion of valorization spaces provokes processes of hyper-exploitation and the destruction of local economies and environment. The demands of profitability imposed by financial capitalism on the entire society reinforce social regression under the high pressure of a growth model that, in order to distribute wealth, voluntarily sacrifices social cohesion and the quality of life itself. Wage deflation, pathologization of labor with increases in health costs generated by work stress (up to 3% of GDP), worsening of social balances, and the irreparable deterioration of the environment are the effects of financial logic and of shareholder delocalizations typical of global financial capitalism.

The *problem* is that, analyzed from a distributive point of view (*economistic* in the last instance), the crisis-development of financial capitalism leads to a veritable dead-end. As it is thrown out the window, i.e., the common place of a kind that is parasitic on finance, it implicitly reenters through the main door. The *impasse*, more theoretical than practico-political, is before everyone's eyes: the impossibility of elaborating strategies to overcome the crisis, the recourse to actions of economic stimulus that, on the one hand, presuppose the rescue of finance (of which we are really hostages), but, on the other hand, annul the very possibilities of economic revival.

Both the right and the left wish for an unlikely return to the real economy, veritable "re-industrializations" of economy (preferably a little greener) in order to leave a financialized economy that is a party to destruction of income and employment. But no one worries anymore about describing the nature and the way of functioning of the so-called "real economy." And thus they wish for state aids to industrial sectors of overproduction, the aids that then are translated into reductions of work positions and wage, which certainly do not help (on the contrary) to revive economy as a whole.

This urgency to return to "making things" reminds us a lot of the critique of the physiocrats addressed to the supporters of the first industrial revolution; the idea, according to which, unlike land products, "machines do not eat," forgets that machines help increase the productivity in that very agricultural center. It may be useful to underscore that countries in commercial surplus, such as the emerging countries, but also Germany and Japan, were able to increase their exports essentially because the countries like the US and England, where the sector of services—not just financial ones—is very developed, have ensured high growth rates of the *demand* of goods and services. And indeed, it is these very countries in commercial surplus that will greatly suffer the effects of the global crisis with the accumulation of enormous overproductions. The fact that the countries in surplus are the ones with the highest rates of savings certainly does not make things simpler: it is indeed true that a reduction of savings could increase the internal demand, but this is exactly what will not happen for the simple reason that the saving will be used to confront the effects of the recession and the stagnation of employment and wages (Simon Tilford, "A Return to 'Making Things' is No Panacea," *Financial Times*, March 4, 2009).

This does not mean that the countries that have, in the last decades, greatly developed the services sector (certainly not just the US and Great Britain) would not have to redefine their own strategies of development on the basis of the crisis itself. But it is not certain that it will be possible to overcome the crisis by returning to an ill-defined "real economy." The countries in commercial deficit, for example, have very high rates of indebtedness in the public and private sectors—an indebtedness, particularly the public one, destined to go up in this period of crisis—but they also have insufficient infrastructures resulting from the years of disinvestment in the sector of public services. Moreover, in these countries, there is a deficit of professional qualifications, a *deficit of valorization* of skills and diffused knowledges that damage, instead of help, knowledge workers.

The real blind spot, both theoretical and practical, has to do with the sterile distinction between manufacturing sector (where they "make things") and the sector of non-material activities, an opposition certainly reinforced by the abnormal development of the financial sector, but one that today risks damaging, in the name of "reindustrialization," all those creative, innovative activities with an added high value that they developed in these last years. It is in activities like these that we have to invest most.

Finally, as if that were not enough, both on the right and on the left, the nationalization of banks in the insolvency crisis is seen as inescapable and/or desirable, without questioning too much into the *social costs* of nationalization, especially when the latter are conceived of as *transitory* actions with a view to the future reprivatization of these very banks. Toxic assets to the State, i.e., to the collectivity, the good banks to the private citizens! This is the usual song: socialize the losses and privatize the benefits (Matthew Richardson, "The Case For and

Against Bank Nationalisation," http://www.voxeu.com/index.php?q=node/3143).

In order to overcome this impasse, it is necessary to analyze critically the crisis of financial capitalism, what it means to begin anew from scratch, i.e., from that increase in profits without accumulation at the root of financialization. Which is to say, it is necessary to analyze financialization as the other side of a process of the value *production* affirmed since the crisis of the Fordist model, i.e., since the capitalist incapacity to suck surplus-value from immediate living labor, the wage labor of the factory. *The thesis that is being put forth here is that financialization is not an unproductive/parasitic deviation of growing quotas of surplus-value and collective saving, but rather the form of capital accumulation symmetrical with new processes of value production.* Today's financial crisis is then interpreted more as a *block* of capital accumulation than an implosive result of a process of lacking capital accumulation.

Apart from the role of finance in the sphere of consumption, what happened in these last 30 years is a veritable metamorphosis of production processes of this very surplus-value. There has been a transformation of valorization processes that witnesses the extraction of value no longer circumscribed in the places dedicated to the production of goods and services, but, so to speak, extending beyond factory gates, in the sense that it enters directly into the sphere of the *circulation* of capital, that is, in the sphere of exchanges of goods and services. It is a question of extending the processes of extracting value from the sphere of reproduction and distribution—a phenomenon, let it be noted, for a long time well known to women. Evermore explicitly, in the center of both theory and managerial strategies, one speaks of the *externalization* of production processes, even of "crowdsourcing," i.e., putting to use the crowd and its forms of life (Jeff Howe, *Crowdsourcing. Why the power of the crowd is driving the future of business*, New York, 2008).

To analyze financial capitalism under this productive profile is to speak of bio-economy or of biocapitalism, "whose form is characterized by its growing entanglement with the lives of human beings. In its precedence, capitalism resorted primarily to the functions of transformation of raw materials carried out by machines and the bodies of the workers. Instead of this, biocapitalism produces value by extracting it not only from the body functioning as the material instrument of work, but also from the body understood in its globality" (Vanni Codeluppi, *Il biocapitalismo. Verso lo sfruttamento integrali di corpi, cervelli ed emozioni*, Bollati Boringhieri, Torino, 2008). In our analysis of the financial crisis, the reference to the whole of the studies and theories of biocapitalism and cognitive capitalism developed in these years is of a merely methodological kind: here we are more interested in highlighting the link between financialization and the processes of value production that is at the basis of the crisis-development of new capitalism than in an accurate and exhaustive description of its salient characteristics (moreover, already accomplished by a growing number of scholars) (The first effort in this sense is the work by Andrea Fumagalli, *Bioeconomia e capitalismo cognitivo*, Carocci, Roma, 2007).

The empirical examples of the externalization of value production, of its extension into the sphere of circulation, are now abundant (of the most recent works on the consumer-as-producer phenomenon, see Marie-Anne Dujarier, *Le travail du consommateur. De McDo à eBay: comment nous coproduisons ce que nous achetons*, La découverte, Paris, 2008). From the first phase of shareholder outsourcing (subcontracts to suppliers and foreign consultants), which, beginning in the 1980s, saw the emergence of atypical labor and of the autonomous labor of the second generation (freelance, entrepreneurs of themselves, former employees who became self-employed) along the same lines as the "Toyota model," the capitalist colonization of the circulation sphere has been nonstop, to the point of transforming the consumer into a veritable producer of economic value. *Coproduction,* where the individual is the coproducer of what he consumes, "is today at the heart of the strategies of public and private companies. The latter put to work the consumer in various phases of value creation. The consumer contributes to creating the market, producing performances, managing damages and hazards, sorting litter, optimizing the fixed assets of suppliers, and even administration. The coproduction concerns all the mass performances and specifically services: retail, bank, transportation, free time, restaurant, media, education, health…" (Durajer, *op. cit.*, p. 8).

It may be useful, even at the risk of simplifying the analysis, to discuss the examples that have since become paradigmatic. Ikea, having delegated to the client a whole series of functions (individuation of the code of the desired item, locating the object, removal of shelves, loading it into the car, etc.), externalizes the labor of assembling the "Billy" bookshelf; that is, Ikea externalizes consistent fixed and variable costs that are now supported by the consumer with a minimal benefit in prices, but with large savings in terms of costs for the company. It is possible to give other examples: the software companies, beginning with Microsoft or Google, usually beta test on the consumers the new versions of their programs, but also the programs belonging to so-called software open source are improved by a multitude of people, by "productive consumers."

After the 2001 crisis, writes Tiziana Terranova, the new strategy of the new economy "is 'social web' or 'web 2.0.' The web 2.0 companies, says

O'Reilly, all have something in common. Their success is based on their capacity to attract masses of users who create a world of social relations on the basis of the platforms/environments made available by sites like Friendster, Facebook, Flickr, My Space, Second Life, and Blogger. Nonetheless, underscores O'Reilly, web 2.0 is not limited to these new platforms, but also involves applications like Google to the extent that they are able to harness and valorize 'browsing' by users; or other applications that once again allow one to extract a surplus-value from common actions such as linking a site, flagging a blog post, modifying a software, and so forth. [...] Web 2.0 is a winning model for investors, since it harnesses, incorporates, and valorizes the social and technological labor of users. The frontier of the innovation of the capitalist valorization process of the new economy is the marginalization of wage labor and the valorization of the 'free labor' of users, i.e., of a labor that is not paid and not supervised, but is nonetheless controlled" (T. Terranova, *New economy, finanziarizzazione e produzione sociale del Web 2.0*, in A. Fumagalli, S. Mezzadra, *op. cit.* The cited work of Tim O'Reilly is *What Is Web 2.0. Design Patterns and Business Models for the Next Generation of Software*, 30/09/2005, http://www.oreillynet.com/pub/a/oreilly/tim/news/2005/09/30/what-is-web-20.html).

The first important consequence of the new processes of capital valorization is the following: the quantity of surplus-value created by new apparatuses of extraction is *enormous*. It is based on the compression of the direct and indirect wage (retirement, social security cushions, earnings from individual and collective savings), on the reduction of socially necessary labor with flexible network company systems (precarization, intermittent employment), and on the creation of vaster pool of free labor (the "free labor" in the sphere of consumption, circulation, and reproduction, with a more intensified cognitive labor). The quantity of surplus-value, i.e., of unpaid labor, is at the root of the increase in the profits *not* reinvested in the production sphere, profits whose increase does not, as a consequence, generate the growth of stable employment, let alone wage.

Under this profile and with a reference to a Marxist debate about the cause of the crisis ("La Brèche"), it is thus possible to partially agree with Alain Bihr's thesis according to which we have for a while been in the presence of an "excess of surplus-value," but, unlike Bihr and Hudson (already cited), this is not the result of a lack of accumulation, of a lack of reinvestment of profits in constant and variable capital. The excess of surplus-value is, *instead*, the result of a *new accumulation process* that took place after the crisis of Fordism *in* the sphere of circulation and reproduction of capital. Francois Chesnais' objections to Alain Bihr's thesis stating that the excess of surplus-value did not just lead to a search for new market outlets—since a significant number of multinational American and European companies have in fact increased their direct investments abroad (in China, Brazil, and, with some difficulties, India)—would thus have to be amplified: direct investments, reflective of the typical seat of capital profit, have not been carried out just outside the economically developed countries, *but right inside*, namely, in the sphere of circulation and reproduction.

The relationship between accumulation, profits, and financialization is reinterpreted on the basis of the salient characteristics of post-Fordist production processes. The increase in profits fueling financialization was possible because, in biocapitalism, the very concept of accumulation of capital was transformed. It no longer consists, as in the Fordist time, of investment in constant and variable capital (wage), but rather of investment in *apparatuses* of producing and capturing value produced outside directly productive processes.

As Tiziana Terranova writes with regard to the new company strategies, "it is a question of attracting and individuating not just this 'free labor,' but also in some way various forms of possible surplus-value that can capitalize on the diffused desires of sociality, expression, and relation. In this model, the production of profit by companies would take place over and against the individuation and capture of a 'lateral' surplus-value (the sale of publicity, and the sale of data produced by the activity of users, the capacity to attract financial investments on the basis of visibility and the prestige of new global brands like Google and Facebook). In many cases, surplus-value resides in the saving of costs of this very labor, since the latter becomes 'externalized' to users (the externalization of analysis and beta testing of videogames or technical support to users)."

These technologies of crowdsourcing, based on what Alexander Galloway called "protocological control," represent the new organic composition of capital, i.e., the relationship between constant capital (as the totality of "linguistic machines") dispersed in society and variable capital (as the totality of sociality, emotions, desires, relational capacity, and... "free labor") deterritorialized, despatialized, dispersed in the sphere of reproduction, consumption, forms of life, individual and collective imagination. The new constant capital, different from the system of (physical) machines typical of the Fordist age, is constituted, apart from information technology and information (TIC), by a totality of non-material organizational systems that suck surplus-value by pursuing citizens in every moment of their lives, with the result that the working day, the time of living labor, is excessively lengthened and intensified (Stephen Baker, "The Next. Companies May Soon Know Where Customers are Likely to be Every Minute of the Day," *Business Week*, March 9, 2009).

The "Google model," like the "Toyota model" 30 years ago, will be properly understood as a new *mode* of producing goods and services in the age of biocapitalism. It is a question of a *model* of company organization that, having assumed the form of internet services in the sector, i.e., in the age of the new economy in the course of the second half of the 1990s, has been gradually asserted in all the sectors of economy, be they producers of non-material services or material goods. In other words, it is not the nature of the product that determined the productive organization (or paradigm), but rather the *relationship* between the production and circulation spheres, between the production and consumption, that shapes the modalities of producing goods and services. The "Google model" is today proposed as a company strategy in order to save the American car industry that made the history of the twentieth century beginning with Henry Ford's revolution and that today is in the gravest crisis from every point of view (Laurent Carroué, "Le couer de l'automobile américaine a cessé de batter," *Le monde diplomatique*, February, 2009).

Jeff Davis' book *What Would Google Do?*, whose excerpt was published by *Business Week* (February 9, 2009), is significant in this regard because it shows how the possibility of overcoming this crisis depends on the capacity of the car industry to reestablish a direct, transparent, participatory, creative, emotive, and expressive relationship with consumers/users of cars. The creation of networks, or, as they are called in the internet world, communities of consumers, who coproduce innovation, diversification, and identification with the brand, on the basis of open source, shows how the "Google model" is asserted outside the virtual universe, even in the hyper-material world of cars. It adds that this managerial revolution began 30 years ago, indeed beginning with the crisis of the Fordist model, a crisis from which one emerged by applying productive strategies that are ever more present in the sphere of circulation and reproduction, i.e., in the sphere of *bios*, of life.

Moreover, the studies of *cognitive capitalism*, (in addition to highlighting the centrality of cognitive/non-material labor, of cooperation between brains beyond the separation of company and territory, between public and private spheres, between individual and organization in the creation of value added), show the increasing loss of strategic importance of fixed capital (*physical* instrumental goods) and the transfer of a series of productive-instrumental functions to the living body of labor-power (Christian Marazzi, *Capitalismo digitale e modello antropogenetico del lavoro. L'ammortamento del corpo macchina*, in J. L. Laville, C. Marazzi, ed. M. La Rosa, F. Chicchi, *Reinventare il lavoro*, Sapere 2000, Rome, 2005).

"The economy of knowledge harbors within itself a curious paradox. The prototype of each new good is costly for the companies because, in order to start producing and commercializing it, huge investments on the level of research are necessary. But the additional units cost little because it is simply a question of replicating the original and it is possible to do this economically thanks to the advantages derived from economies of scale, from available technologies, and digitalization processes. It follows that companies will concentrate their efforts and resources on the production of ideas, having to confront, however, the progressive tendency of the increase in costs" (Codeluppi, *op. cit.*, p. 24).

One of the main characteristics of cognitive capitalism is, in fact, the chasm between initially very high costs (particularly due to the investments in Research and Development, marketing, etc) necessary for continued invention/innovation of products and marginal costs of additional units of products introduced to the market, the costs tending to zero. Being able to be replicated at decreasing costs lies in fact in the very nature of products of high technological content and cognitive labor (on this subject, see the fundamental work by E. Rullani, *Economia della conoscenza. Creatività e valore nel capitalismo delle reti*, Carocci, Roma, 2004. Also important is the work *L'età del capitalismo cognitivo. Innovazione, proprietà e cooperazione delle moltitudini,* ed. by Yann Moulier Boutang, Ombre Corte, Verona, 2002).

This characteristic of cognitive capitalism refers to the theory of *growing earnings*, i.e., to the increase in profits originated in the drastic reduction of reproduction costs of goods. The theory of growing earnings, particularly relevant in an economy that has turned knowledge into a highly productive and competitive factor of production (*endogenous*, i.e., the integral part of the *normal* activity of companies), was masterly examined by David Warsh in his *La conoscenza e la ricchezza delle nazioni. Una storia dell'indagine economica* (Feltrinelli, Milano, 2006).

In the end of our analysis, it will suffice to reiterate the example of the "pin factory" so much used by the economists in order to explain the increase in the productivity of labor resulting from the division-specialization of labor. "Let us suppose," writes Warsh, "that our pin factory immediately enters the market and after a period of expansion is further specialized, investing in new machines, researching and developing in the field of pins. It has developed the best steel, most attractive packaging, developed a most effective retail network. The bigger the market, the further it is possible to go on the road of specialization: it is possible to replace workers with new machines and, thanks to the increase in efficiency, lower the sales prices on pins. The more one is able to keep the prices low, the more pins are sold and the better is the profit, which in essence means having a better earning with the same effort, i.e., a proportionally growing earning" (pp. 69–70).

Analyzed under this profile, Adam Smith's "pin factory" (that very much reminds us of today's multinational companies) evokes the tendency of the companies possessing the know-how accumulated in machines and living labor towards monopoly, that is, a situation where the first to arrive gets everything and the market is resupplied with pins "perhaps not in the quantity as to satisfy the demand." Something is in strident contradiction with the other (still major) interpretation of Adam Smith, according to which the "invisible hand," that is, the *free* competition, is governing the market such that "no producer can prevail and if someone tries to increase the prices, he is at once cut out, such that the price immediately returns to its 'natural value': there are as many pins on the market as needed by consumers." In other words, "the pin factory speaks of reduction of costs and increasing earnings. The invisible hand speaks, instead, of increase in costs and decreasing earnings" (p. 70), and the two theorems, naturally, exclude each other.

However, the increasing earnings are counterbalanced by the continued tendency of increasing production costs determined by a series of other factors, such as the growth of market exchange rates, the rapid technological obsolescence of productive facilities, the increased requests of consumers, the necessity of producing always new stimuli in order to incite the desire of wealthy consumers, the growth of the competition rate between companies, the competition between company messages and other messages circulating in society, the growing complexity of the social system (Codeluppi, *op. cit.*, pp. 25–26).

In order to confront the rise of costs, companies develop both forms of externalization of entire segments of activity in countries with low cost of labor, as well as processes of the creation of *scarcity* (by means of certificates, patents, copyrights) necessary to recoup the initial costs with the prices of monopolistic sales. Finally, they develop the reduction of direct investment in capital assets. For example, in order to reduce the initial costs, the companies "no longer think of purchasing capital assets, but of borrowing, through various forms of hire contracts, the physical capital they need, deducting both relative costs and exercise costs in the same manner as a cost of activity" (Jeremy Rifkin, *L'era dell'accesso. La rivoluzione della new economy*, Mondadori, Milano, p. 57).

The increase in the quantity of living labor not only reflects the transfer of the strategic means of production (consciousness, knowledges, cooperation) in the living body of labor-power, but allows one to explain the trend loss of the economic value of the classical means of production. It is thus not a mystery if the recourse to stock markets in all these years is not aimed at the investments immediately productive of an increase in the amount of employment and wage, but rather at the increase in shareholder value pure and simple. The auto-financing of investments in fixed capital assets and wage, should there be any, shows that the accumulation leverage has something to do with the monetization of value produced outside companies, i.e., inside society.

The increase in profits over the last 30 years is thus due to a production of surplus-value *by* accumulation, although an accumulation entirely unforeseen because it is external to classical productive processes. It is in this sense that the idea of "rent becoming rent" (and, in part, wage itself) is justified as a result of the capture of a value produced outside directly productive spaces. Today's system of production curiously resembles the eighteenth century economic circuit centered around farming and theorized by the physiocrats. In Quesnay's *Tableau économique*, rent represents the quota of the net product, appropriated by the landlord, generated by agricultural labor of wage workers (including the labor of the capitalist tenant where income was considered in the same way as the wage of his workers and not, as it later will be defined by Smith and Ricardo, as profit). In the *Tableau*, the physical instruments of production are not even taken into consideration. Quesnay defined the producers of instrumental goods (constant capital) as the active part of the *sterile* class, that is, not productive of net product, to the extent that the production of instruments of labor does not add anything to the raw material used, but only *transforms* it.

The exclusion of constant capital, instrumental goods, from the factors of production of net product was certainly a mistake, as was later shown by the fathers of classical political economy on the wave of the first industrial revolution. The physiocrats' mistake was to consider as productive exclusively agricultural labor, the only labor that, producing things with things, is quantitatively *measurable*. But it is a mistake that is *productive of knowledge*, if it is true the subsequent discovery of economic value of constant capital and its qualitative difference with respect to variable capital—that is, the discovery of *generic labor*, the labor *abstracted from* specific sectors where it is carried out—was at the basis of the epistemological leap that radically distinguished modernity from capitalism. That is, the qualitative-subjective *separation* between capital and labor, the contradictory *relationship* between the two "factors of production" as the leverage of *crisis-development* of nascent capitalism. From that moment on, capitalism has been developing *following* the subjective rearticulations of living labor, its struggles, its aspirations, and its unforeseen forms of cooperation.

It is possible to say that the forms of life weakening the social body are equivalent to land in Ricardo's theory of rent. Only that, unlike Ricardo's rent (absolute and differential), today's rent is subsumable under the very profit *by virtue* of financialization processes themselves. The financialization, with the logics defining it—particularly the autonomization of the production of money via money by the directly productive processes—is the other side of externalization of the value production typical of biocapitalism. This does not just contribute to the production of the effective demand necessary for the *realization* of the product of surplus-value, i.e., does not just create the amount of rent and consumption without which the growth of GDP would be low and stagnant. Rather, financialization fundamentally *determines* continuous innovations, continuous leaps that are productive of biocapitalism, thus imposing on all companies, quoted or not, and on the whole society its hyper-productive logics centered around the primacy of shareholder value. The productive leaps determined by financialization are systematically carried out by "creative destructions" of capital, by successive extensions of valorization processes at the very heart of society with ever more sophisticated models of crowdsourcing. By crises ever more frequent and reconciled, crises where access to social wealth, after having been stimulated, is from time to time destroyed.

Starting with the crisis of Fordism in the 1970s, economic bubbles are thus interpreted as moments of crisis within a long-term process of "capitalist colonization" of the circulation sphere. This process is *globalized*, that is, a process of subsuming growing quotas of global and local socio-economic peripheries in accordance with the logic of financial (bio)capitalism. The passage from imperialism to empire, i.e., from a relationship of dependence between development and underdevelopment where the economies of the South functioned as *external* market outlets in addition to being the sources of downmarket raw material, to imperial globalization where the dichotomy between inside and outside breaks down, is also to be included in the capitalist logic of the externalization of the value production processes. *Financialization represents the adequate and perverse modality of accumulation of new capitalism.*

4

A CRISIS OF GLOBAL GOVERNANCE

Beginning in August 2007 with the explosion of sub-prime loans, the financial crisis looks evermore like a long-term crisis, a crisis paired with credit crunch, banking bankruptcies, continued interventions of monetary authorities not able to influence the structuring of the crisis; there are evermore costly actions of economic revival, risks of insolvency of individual countries, deflationary pressures and possible violent returns of inflation, increase in unemployment and income reduction. For all intents and purposes, this crisis is *historical*, in the sense that it contains all the contradictions accumulated over the course of the gradual financialization of economy that began with the crisis of the Fordist way of accumulation (for an analysis of the deregulation of the banking system that began in 1970s in the midst of the Fordist crisis, see Barry Eichengreen, "Anatomy of the Financial Crisis," *Vox*, http://www.voxeu.org/index.php?q=node/1684).

Nevertheless, the present crisis finds in the Asian crisis of 1997–1999 its moment of determination and acceleration. Certainly, the Asian crisis was, in turn, preceded by a series of foreboding crises, such as the

Mexican and Argentinian crises, the Russian and Brazilian crises, the crisis of Long Term Capital Management, the Japanese "lost decade," crises that Paul Krugman analyzed in 1998 in his *Il ritorno dell'economia della depressione*, republished in 2008 with an update on the subprime loan crisis and the general banking crisis. However, the Asian crisis marked a change of regime in the international financial order from the moment the Southern and Asian countries decided—in order to overcome the crisis of excessive debt in dollars that caused real estate speculation and industrial overinvestment in local currency—to accumulate reserves of international currencies to protect themselves against the risk of subsequent destructive crises in the instability of monetary and world financial system. It is a question of a radical change in the economic model, to the extent that, from a growth increased by internal demand, the Asian countries chose a model of growth based on exports. In this way, the Asian countries went from being dollar debtors to creditors, particularly in the US. In order to accumulate foreign currencies, the Asian countries adopted the "predatory" policy in international commerce, resorting to strong devaluations, a policy of competitive deflation, and the limitation of internal consumption. If this is what the opening of international commerce in countries like China and India intends, the net result of an Asian turn is understood as a deflationary kind:

certainly for wages, which suddenly redouble the world amount of active population, but deflationary also for industrial consumer goods produced and exported from China and, to a lesser yet qualitatively important extent, from India. The wage deflation "was, on the other hand, strongly aggravated by the eruption of financial logics in the companies in the real sector of economy, by procedure like reacquisition of companies through debt and leverage effect (the leveraged buy-out or LBO)" (Sapir, *op. cit.*, p. 5).

The risk of deflation is revealed as evermore real after the internet bubble crisis. In fact, since 2007, the debt redemption of companies, which have accumulated debts in the expansive period of the internet bubble (1998–2000), compels Alan Greenspan's Federal Reserve to pursue an expansive monetary policy. In order to avoid entering the vicious circle of deflation experienced by Japan in the 1990s, the American monetary authorities decide to keep interest rates low (around 1%) for a particularly long period, because, with a view to company bankruptcies (Enron, to name just one) called in since 2002, the expansive monetary policy cannot reestablish the confidence of stock markets. In any case, *negative* real interest rates reinforce private indebtedness, but, at the same time, cause banks to develop in order to increase the credit amount, the panoply of financial instruments and the famous securitizations under accusation today (the now famous toxic assets).

The subprime real estate bubble begins in this context. Companies manage, at least partially, to redeem their debt thanks to negative real interest rates, while the domestic American economies become exponentially indebted (very often *urged* to go in debt). The increase in consumption by debt aggravates the American commercial deficit and, consequently, reinforces, even more, the monetary mercantilist policies of the Asian countries (who, by buying massive amounts of dollars in order to avoid devaluation which would damage their exports to the US and create Sovereign Funds through the budget excesses, also sterilize their realized gains; these state funds will, for a certain period, seem to able to resolve the crisis of the Western banks). The deflationary tendency is also aggravated because the commercial excesses of the Asian countries (despite the actions of sterilization) generate investments in these very exporting countries; the investments that, in turn, improve the competitiveness of the emerging countries not only through the low labor cost, but also through the quality of products and the higher added value.

The description, however schematic, of the dynamic that led to the subprime bubble burst shows that the crisis ripened within a precise *world* configuration of the capitalist accumulation process. Within this configuration and this international division of labor, financialization allowed *global* capital to grow thanks to the production of financial rents and consumer debts that endowed international exchanges with *systemic coherence*. The global growth, particularly after the internet bubble crisis and debt redemption on the part of companies following it, witnessed capital restructure itself with subsequent externalization processes. The aim here is to reduce the cost of living labor with increases in the quantity of surplus-value, the increases not correlated with increases proportional to investments in constant capital. In fact, particularly from 1998 to 2007, the large companies (S&P 500) witnessed a continued and particularly high increase in non-reinvested profits (free cash flow margins), an accumulation of liquidity parallel to the increase of consumption, either with reduced family savings or with recourse to indebtedness.

As always, the crises of capital break loose because of the same forces that determined their growth (the typical palindromic movement of the transaction cycle). But *this* crisis illuminates something unforeseen with regard to the preceding crises—which is the loss of capacity on the part of American monetary authorities, (even if they manage the international currency par excellence), to manage liquidities arriving at their market as a result of the "mercantilist"-predatory monetary strategy used in the Asian countries since the '97–'99 crisis. This specificity (in his day, Alan Greenspan spoke of "conundrum"), already pointed out by Michel

Aglietta and Laurent Berrebi (*Désordres dand le capitalisme mondial*, Odile Jacob, Paris, 2007), refers to the consequences of a liquidity influx from the emerging countries and from the countries producing and exporting gasoline to the American bond market—particularly Treasury bonds and Fannie Mae and Freddie Mac's obligations. The massive and continued liquidity influx from the emerging countries in fact *reduces* long-term interest rates on bonds, such as T-bills. In fact, when bonds giving a fixed income increase in value because they are in high demand on the market, corresponding interest rates decrease proportionately in order to be able to ensure the same earning.

The reduction of long-term interest rates occurs *despite* the Fed's repeated attempts between 2004 and 2007 to restrain the increase in the amount of credits with the increase in direct, short-term interest rates (that jump from 1% to 5.25%). "It is this very special situation of inverted curve where long-term interest rates have become less than short-term rates—situation atypical for such a long period—that made it so that the credit cost remained very low for quite some time in the US, despite an evermore restrictive monetary policy" (Aglietta, *La crise*, p. 39). Being able to give out loans to wholesale money markets, the banks thus have the means to give out credits with an ever higher risk to the domestic economies. Consequently, real estate prices in the US were rising until the fall of

2006 and until 2008 in various European countries (in France, rising from 60% to 80%, in England and Spain redoubling over ten years).

The crisis of governance of the American monetary authorities is thus explained as the incapacity to manage the effects of liquidity influx from the rest of the world, especially from the emerging countries. In fact, the post-crisis Asian globalization *obscures* within the developed countries the increase in risk of crisis internal to the transaction cycle, because the reduction of premiums on the bonds risks (long-term bonds) reinforces the exposition of the financial sector to the valorization of all patrimonial assets. Once again, in this process, it is the *temporal dimension* that is central in the analysis of the crisis. The signs of a real estate crisis were manifesting themselves already since 2004, so much that the Fed began its race to increase interest rates. But the influx of foreign liquidity annulled the actions of monetary policy so that the bubble was unfolding undeterred until August 2007. And not just that: already in the middle of 2006, real estate prices halted their rise to then drop towards the end of the same year. But the bubble exploded in August 2007 when the rating agencies finally decided to declassify (now toxic) assets issued in credit; which is to say, a year after the inversion of the transaction cycle (to confirm this reconstruction of the post-Asian crisis, see, "When a Flow Becomes a Flood," *The Economist,* January 24, 2009).

In other words, the crisis of monetary governance reveals a *gap* between the economic and financial-monetary cycles, in the sense that the former develops in a shorter time than the latter. In the cycle of the real economy, like in all business cycles, the crisis begins at the moment when the inflationary increase in prices (for example, of real estate) provokes a *falling* increase of demand. The demand grows, but grows ever more slowly because actualizing the flow of future incomes no longer justifies the "irrational" increase in prices on goods on which the bubble is concentrated.

In the "old" economic cycles, this slowdown was usually manifested by near-full employment. For the banking system, this means a slowdown in the rhythm of repaying the credits lavished in the phase preceding the cycle, the phase during which credit is easy and super-speculation is unleashed on the wave of the increase in profits (the so-called financial overtrading). In approaching the full employment, companies and indebted consumers are, however, showing signs of difficulty repaying their debts because the amount of sales (for the companies struggling with the drop of demand) and available incomes (for the domestic economies confronted by inflation) begins to fall. For the banks, from the secondary to the central ones, this is the moment to increase the interest rates.

The overtrading and super-speculation preceding the inversion of the transaction cycle are nothing other than the creation of an earning *extrinsic* to the production of goods and services, of a demand *additional* to the one created directly inside the economic circuit. Overtrading reinforces the spending of a virtual income quite a lot by anticipating its realization. Under this profile, the multiplication of securitized assets has certainly been at the basis of overtrading, to the extent that it allowed for the creation of virtual incomes on the basis of the presupposition, later revealed as entirely unrealistic, of a future realization. But when overtrading topples over into its opposite, that is, when it goes from the phase of easy money to one characterized by credit crunch, this additional demand collapses, it vaporizes very quickly, and the economic system enters into recession. Companies in every sector are no longer able to sell, warehouses accumulate more and more supplies, and the domestic economies begin to experience the reduction of their income due to dismissals and/or the difficulty maintaining consumption at the same levels as those of the preceding phase of the cycle. This is the moment when the crisis is revealed as the crisis of *overproduction* on an enlarged scale. This is also the moment when, in order to reestablish an operative balance between demand and supply, one very often turns to *scrapping* of unsold surplus or, in any case, to its devalorization. The violence of crises consists in this *destruction of capital*, a destruction that in biocapitalism strikes the totality of human beings, their emotions, feelings, affects, that is, all the "resources" put to work by the capital (for a description of the role of finance in the expansion-recession dynamic of the economic cycle based on Hyman Minsky's theory, see Robert Barbera, *The Cost of Capitalism: Understanding Markez Mayhem and Stabilising Our Economic Future*, McGraw-Hill, 2009).

The collapse of overtrading manifests itself in its entire *social* dimension, i.e., as a phenomenon of *realization*, of selling the quantity of goods and services (and the quantity of value embodied in them) that concerns not just one sector or another (if this were the case, we would be present at an inter-sectorial compensation), but *all* the sectors at once. But the fact that the overturning of super-speculation—that is, the crunch to the point of zeroing the additional demand created by the mechanism of overtrading— is at the root of overproduction also shows that the imbalance between demand and supply is a *structural* characteristic of the economic cycle. In other words, the supply of goods and services is *at the root* of excessive demand. Say's law, postulating a fundamental identity between supply and demand, is thus false, not just because the explosion of the crisis involves rushing to banking windows and the deferral of spending on the part of the domestic economies (so-called retention), but also because demand and supply are structurally in imbalance. If this were the case, the collapse of overtrading would have to reestablish the equality between demand and supply—something that never happens. The crisis reveals the excess of supply over demand, latent overproduction inside the transaction cycle. It is for this reason that the crisis calls into being anti-cyclical actions tending to create new additional demand, actions that only the State can implement, since there is a general flight in the private economy. No mechanism of market autoregulation can alone reestablish the conditions for overcoming the crisis.

Financial globalization, as we saw, *defers* the rendering of accounts, that is, the inversion of the cycle, precisely because the amount of credit to companies and consumers can keep increasing despite the signs of the inversion of the real internal economy cycle (for instance, the prices on real estate beginning to drop). All of this despite the trend in the balance of payments that contributes to obscuring the symptoms of the imminent crisis. In fact, until the massive influx of savings from the emerging countries, in search of not high, but secure earnings, is counterbalanced by the flow of American investments directed abroad (which have earnings greater than the internal ones and which increase the profits of US companies, especially when the dollar is low relative to other currencies), the American monetary authorities can avoid confronting the *all the while evident* problem of the international commercial imbalances.

Moreover, the temporal gap, where the crisis of American monetary governance is reversed, is at the root of the transformation of regional crises into *immediately* global ones. Certainly, this, is due to the dissemination of risks and toxic assets that in this period, infects bank portfolios, insurances, hedge and equity funds, retirement funds, and everyone's investments. But, at a closer look, it is a question of a crisis that goes well beyond the world diffusion of toxic assets. This is shown by the total inefficiency of all the actions of intervention undertaken up to now by the governments in all over the world in order to recapitalize the banking and insurance system through the huge injections of liquidity.

It is thus possible to claim that the crisis of monetary governance explains *only* one part, only the *beginning* of the crisis we are living in. What proves it is that, at the worst moment of the financial crisis—October 2008—contrary to what everyone expected, the dollar was *revalued* against all the other currencies. "The anomaly is that the dollar is reinforced over the course of these last weeks against almost all other currencies" (Eichengreen, *op. cit.*). But it can happen that, like after the reevaluation of the dollar in August 2007 (in the midst of the subprime crisis!), the dollar starts to devalue again, with inevitable inflationary effects on a world scale (caused, like over the course of 2007–2008, by strong increases in the prices on gasoline and food). It is possible that the global imbalances between the structurally deficient countries (the US and England), and the countries structurally in surplus, such as the emerging countries (but also Germany and Japan), are destined to still last a long time. A long time, i.e., *beyond* the rescue actions and the redefinition of the banking and financial rules that—from the internet crisis until the subprime bubble burst—allowed the flow of liquidity towards the US to produce the leverage effect of credit that we saw. As a high official of the China Bank Regulatory Commission, Luo Ping, told a journalist of the *Financial Times*, "we hate you guys, but there is nothing much we can do" except continue to buy American public debt (cited in Bill Powell, "China's Hard Landing," *Fortune*, March 16, 2009).

It would suffice to pose a seemingly provocative question: What else could the American monetary authorities and the rest of the world do? Certainly, with hindsight, it is possible to say anything; it is possible, for instance, to invoke (precisely *ex post*) prudential monetary policies, increases in banking reserves, better quality control of issued assets, stricter rules on securitizations based on subprime mortgage loans, and so on. But what could have the American monetary authorities and the central banks of the emerging countries have done, the former being confronted with the risk of deflation, the latter recovering, shattered, from the '97–'99 crisis? The answer is: Nothing other than what has been done. It suffices to say that if the Fed had effected a more restrictive monetary policy in order to restrain or lessen the foreign deficit of the current balance, the result would have been a recession in the US and, consequently, in the emerging countries as well. On top of that, how could the Fed have justified a restrictive monetary policy when the problem was not inflation, but rather deflation?

Let us only recall that a peculiar characteristic of today's financial capitalism and the monetary policy proper to it is the impossibility of managing from outside what occurs inside the economico-financial cycle. The theoretical analyses of André Orléan, Michel Aglietta, Robert Shiller, Hyman Minsky, George Soros, and Frédéric Lordon, to cite the best, show that, how, in order to interpret the behavior of financial operators on the basis of the value-at-risk models, it is impossible to distinguish between cognitive and manipulative functions, between economic rationality and mimetic behavior of the multiplicity of actors. The neo-classical theory of rational expectations, based on perfect information and the transparency of markets, has, for a long time, been beside the point, because it removes a central factor of the financial markets, i.e., the intrinsic *uncertainty* characteristic of them, an uncertainty evermore based on the diminishing dichotomy between real and financial economies. In other words, the hypothesis of "efficient markets" has to be substituted by that of "market instability," a structural instability within the public nature of currency, as "public good," engineering collective behaviors (such as panic) that have little to do with the rationality of individual economic operators, but that are, however, integral part of the market functioning.

According to George A. Akerlof and Robert Shiller, the rationality of *Homo economicus* explains only a quarter of relevant economic actions. The rest is guided by animal spirits already described by Keynes, i.e., it is the aptitude of individuals to "flirt with ambiguity" which guides decisions about investments when uncertainty prevents one from being rational (*Animal Spirits. How Human Psychology Drives the Economy and Why it Matters for Global Capitalism*, Princeton University Press, Princeton, 2009). "These non-economic motivations are mood-related and subject to spontaneous changes that drag economy up and down. If rationality is a good guide in normal times, it is less so in situations of positive (economic bubbles) and negative (crises) stress. We neither anticipated the crisis nor are we able to overcome it because we do not take this factor into account" (Giorgio Barba Navaretti, *Travolti dagli Animal Spirits*, "Il Sole 24 Ore," March 8, 2009). That the times have not been normal for a while now shows that, from 1985 until today, i.e., from the liberal turn imparted to the economies by market deregulation, there has been a financial and/or monetary crisis, on average, every two and half years. This is enough to definitively put in crisis the fundamental presuppositions of the neo-classical theory, according to which "markets realize the best allocation of capital and the best management of risk."

In fact, there is a particular ontological weakness in the models of probability calculation used to evaluate risks due to the *endogenous* nature of the interactions between the financial operators (see André Orléan, *La notion de valeur fondamentale est-elle indispensable à la théorie financière?, Regards croisés sur l'économie. Comprendre la finance contemporaine,* March 3, 2008). It is what explains the "mistakes of evaluation" of risk not so much, or not only, as mistakes attributable to the conflict of interests typical of rating agencies, but as the expression of an (ontological) impossibility of making rules or meta-rules in order to be able to discipline the markets in accordance with so-called rational principles. All the more so when, according to the methods used to establish the value of financial assets, like the ones based on the new accounting norms (International Financial Reporting Standards, IFRS, secured by Basel II), the fair value of assets is calculated on the basis of the conflict between their market value and the one at which the asset is being negotiated, that is, its historical value (the method used to establish this valuation is called 'mark to market'). The problem posed by these methods of valuation is that, from the moment when fair values start to function in reference to the calculation of value of a patrimonial asset—in the same way as a private citizen who calculates his *real* estate, including the *current* market value of his real estate—there is a strong urge to increase asset value by increasing debt: "in an accounting of this kind, the debt of assets buyers seems weak because it is guaranteed, collaterally, by assets whose value grows faster than debt. Thus, bankers do not understand the risk because they see market values as indicators. But this risk, nonetheless very real, does not at all appear in the variables that are measured on the basis of accounting rules considered a good standard" (Aglietta, *op. cit.*, pp. 18–19). It is a question of a veritable urge to indebtedness, precisely as it occurs over the course of the period of the greatest economic financialization. *And this is according to the very rules established on the international level of a kind that is supposed to regulate the markets!*

It is possible to maintain that the crisis of governance has its origin in a double resistance: on the one hand, the resistance of the emerging countries to every attempt to keep them in the subordinate position with respect to the developed countries, a resistance that led them to modify their growth model after the Asian crisis. The Asian export-oriented model has in fact transformed the amount of savings not reinvested internally into *financial rent*—the rent realized by redirecting liquidity towards the outside; on the other hand, there has been the resistance of the American domestic economies that have played the card of *social rent*, a kind of "with and against" the financialization of economy. For a certain period of time, American families were acting, in however financially unstable form, on the terrain of social property rights, the right to the house and the (indebted) consumption of goods and services. And this was, we would do well to recall, in a period of the state disinvestment in the fundamental sectors such as education and professional training, the disinvestment that caused the impressive increase in the cost of education, forcing families to go in debt in order to allow their own children to study. The private spending deficit, far from being the reflection of an all-American tendency to live beyond one's own means, is a phenomenon that has its roots in the liberal turn in the beginning of the 1980s and in the crisis of the Welfare State that followed it (on this subject, see Colin Crouch, "What Will Follow the Demise of Privatised Keynesianism," *The Political Quarterly*, No. 4, October–December 2008).

5

GEOMONETARY SCENARIOS

The crisis is the capitalist way of transferring to the economic order the social and potentially political dimension, the dimension of the resistances ripened during the phase leading up to the cycle. However, this crisis exploded on the basis of such a tangle of contradictions and rigidity on a global scale that the Keynesian actions of intervention on a regional scale are hardly able to undo them. It is thus obvious that the overcoming of the crisis is possible only if the actions of economic revival are inscribed in precise geopolitical and geomonetary strategies.

There are, essentially, three medium-term (from 5 to 10 years) scenarios which are extrapolated from the current crisis: "The first is founded on the US-China coupling (Chimerica), thus on a pact between the dollar and yuan. The second extends the game to Russia and Euro-Western powers, Germany and France come to mind, bound by a special agreement between Euroland and ruble (Eurussia). Thus determining, parallel to the Chino-American axis, the premises of a super Bretton Woods, a full agreement between all the major powers. The third scenario is the exacerbation of imbalances (beginning with the old Europe mayonnaise going bad and ongoing conflicts) to the point of rendering the system completely ungovernable. The catastrophes pile up to then reproduce August 1914, this time on a nuclear and planetary scale" (Lucio Caracciolo "L'impera senza credito," *Limes*, 5, 2008).

All these scenarios are based upon the inevitability of the decline of American hegemony, the decline of the *empire without credit*, the formula describing the paradox of the largest world power that is also the largest global debtor; they are based on the "self-evident" hypothesis that is to be legitimately doubted if it is true that the crisis strikes the Asian countries in a particularly grave way, from China to Singapore, from Japan to South Korea ("Asia's Suffering," *The Economist*, January 31, 2009), while the US continues to be, as paradoxical as it may seem, one of the most secure places to invest one's savings.

Today's crisis ripened within a complex geo-monetary order that witnessed the multiplicity of actors bound to one another by autoreferential interests. China can maintain that the Americans would have to save the most, but only as long as the major saving does not affect its exports to the US. And the Americans can ask the Chinese how they managed, repeatedly in the past and, evermore timidly, even now, to reevaluate their currency and increase their internal consumption, but Americans are wary of restraining the purchase of T-bills by the Chinese. On the other hand, this crisis is already provoking a strong reduction in the net flow of private capital to the emerging countries (in 2009, it will not exceed $165 billion, at least in the half of $466 billion of 2008 and a fifth of the capital flow of 2007). For their part, the actions of tax stimulus and of rescuing the bankrupt Western banks can only produce the crowding out of the emerging markets and those of Eastern Europe. These actions would thus increase, on top of all of that, their public debt service. Which, let it be noted, can cause some Asian countries to try to protect themselves by increasing their currency reserves still more and investing their savings in the debt of the more developed economies, reiterating in such a way the same dynamics that prepared the explosion of credit in the US. In other words, the fundamental imbalances at the root of the crisis-development of financial capitalism of recent years are destined to persist for quite a lot of time, as Martin Wolf maintains on the pages of *Financial Times* ("Why G20 leaders will fail to deal with the big challenge," *FT*, April 1, 2009).

Thus, it is not the decline of the American empire that compels one to try the way of international cooperation in order to better manage the global imbalances, but rather the fact that this crisis is destined to last a long time without any country being able to assume the role of the leader of the world economy. As David Brooks said in an article that appeared in *Herald Tribune*, August 2, 2008, in today's global system, that which paralyzes capitalism is the impossibility of decision. The dispersion of power "should, in theory, be a good thing, but in practice, multipolarity means that more groups have effective veto power over collective action. In practice, this new pluralistic world has given rise to globosclerosis, an inability to solve problem after problem." In other words, the crisis radically undermined the very concept of unilateral and multi-lateral economico-political hegemony, i.e., that which compels one to explore new forms of multilateral world governance.

The first step in this direction is to ensure the emerging countries, and not just the Asian ones, that in case of a liquidity crisis they will not be left alone. The offer, in October, on the Fed's part of a line of credit to four emerging countries, even though these same countries already had abundant reserves, is interpreted as an innovation in this direction. The objective is to best coordinate the actions of political economy to reorient the flows of capital so as to stim-ulate the internal demand in the emerging countries, without, however, jeopardizing the monetary balance between the dollar and other currencies. It is worth noting that this strategy includes the countries in the European zone, since Germany is also structurally in commercial excess and thus has all the interest to pursue policies of a revival of internal demand in order to counteract the drop of the external demand.

We should also note that the implementation of this geopolitico-monetary strategy witnesses, for the time being, the IMF play an entirely marginal role. The amounts in play well exceed the financial availability of the Fund. As a matter of fact, in the medium-long term, such an operative reinvention of the IMF (most importantly, a consistent increase in its liquidity, as the increase of $500 billion decided on by the G20 and an internal redistribution of power from the US to the emerging countries) will reveal itself as necessary for the simple reason that the US cannot guarantee in the medium term to help the emerging countries with "precautionary" lines of credit. The construction of a super Bretton Woods with the IMF as its new armed hand, repeatedly invoked by the French President Sarkozy, must reckon with a characteristic of the Fund that sums up the gist of neoliberal American politics in the last decades.

It is a question of writing, highly valued in the US, into the statutes of the Fund, the obligation to the convertibility into a capital account (a convertibility that Keynes, during the preparatory work on the Bretton Woods agreements, resisted with all his force) where before there was only the convertibility into a current account. "And yet, the difference between the two notions is thus essential. In the second, the accent is on the flows of currencies that cover real transactions, on exchanges of goods and services, on tourist flows or the ones that still correspond to the repatriation of the incomes of the immigrants. In the first notion, all the portfolio operations, all the possible instruments of speculation, are authorized" (Sapir, *op. cit.*, p. 3).

The idea of a super Bretton Woods would be to cancel the obligation to convert into a capital account. This convertibility since the 1980s represented a precondition of the liberation processes of the international markets and of the accumulation of global imbalances that repeatedly produced the financial crises of the last 30 years. Today the same IMF recognizes that this freedom of movement of capital significantly contributed to the destabilization of the system of commercial exchanges and international financial flows. However, the removal of the convertibility obligation into a capital account from the statutes of a hypothetical new IMF—that has as its fundamental objective the reestablishment of the *economic sovereignty* of nations and the symmetry of exchange relations guaranteed by a supranational monetary system—would have the inevitable consequence of disabling the apparatus that ensured, although with an impressive accumulation of contradictions and financial drifts, the development and affirmation of financial biocapitalism.

For the sake of beginning, the US would no longer be able to profit from the massive liquidity influx from the emerging countries which, as we saw, allowed American capital to explode consumption through the debt of American families. However one values the hypothesis of a new Bretton Woods, it is certain that a reform of it in this sense would have spectacular effects on a model of society that, having dismantled the Welfare State, turned consumption and private indebtedness into the motor of its *modus operandi*. "The breaking point between the partisans of the old disorder and the partisans of a real reconstruction of the financial monetary system will be concentrated on two questions: the control of capital and of the forms of protectionism that allow one to avoid importing the depressive effects of the policies of some countries" (Sapir, *op. cit.*, p. 32).

For the moment, the willingness of the Chinese government to continue purchasing assets of the American State does not seem to be in question (over the last years, China purchased 2 trillion of dollars in American T-bills), but the same Chinese government voiced the hypothesis of a radical reform of the international monetary system in order to escape from the "trap of the dollar," that is, from the real risk of one of its devaluations (on this subject, see Zhou Xiuaochuan, governor of the central Chinese bank, *Reform the International Monetary System*, http://www.pbc.gov.cn/english). "The Chinese willingness," wrote Alfonso Tuor, "has, however, a price and this price is very high, especially for the US. Peking asks for the reform of the international monetary system (a new Bretton Woods) with the objective to create a supranational exchange currency in the place of the dollar. The Chinese authorities think that this function could be accomplished by the Special Drawing Rights of the IMF" ("Chi pagherà il conto della crisi?," *Corriere del Ticino*, March 27, 2009). Despite the hypothesis of reform, the mere call to which has immediately destabilized the dollar on the currency markets, which is to be understood in gradual terms, it is clear that this would entail the loss of the hegemony of the American currency in favor of the institution of a supranational currency (Special Drawing Rights), a synthetic monetary unity constituted by a totality of national currencies.

However, let it be recalled that the Special Drawing Rights are not a real supranational currency, but rather a unity of account comprised of other national currencies (dollar, euro, yen, and sterling). Which means that the idea of escaping from the trap of the dollar in which China finds itself after years of investing its own currency reserves in American T-bills can only be understood as desire on the part of the Chinese monetary authorities to *diversify* their own currency reserves, in other words, to reduce the detention of the dollar in favor of other national currencies, such as the euro, the yen, or the sterling. The reduction of the dollar detention would entail the devaluation of the American currency, a devaluation that would certainly damage Chinese exports. The fact that, at least at the moment, neither the Chinese nor the Americans discuss the fundamental imbalance between the countries in export surplus and the developed countries in deficit (US and UK) renders a reform of the international monetary system highly problematic on this basis.

As Joseph Halevi wrote, commenting on the results of the G20 summit in London on April 2, "in the *Financial Times* of March 31, Martin Wolf established with simplest criterion for evaluating the decisions of the G20. Are these countries able to displace the redistribution of the world demand from the countries in deficit to the ones in surplus to make them spend and import? Wolf's hypothesis, which revealed itself to be right, was that this was not even attempted. As the New York Times notes, the meeting approved, by means of the IMF, funds in case of crisis of payment on the part of the developing countries and the line of credit equaling $1100 billion. It did not, however, launch any direct action to stimulate the demand. The G20 thus were not politically in the position to address the crucial knot put forward by Wolf. To undo it, however, we need to break the wage deflation in Europe and reorient the productive structures of both Japan and China" ("Il summit e i conflitti intercapitalistici," *Il manifesto*, April 4, 2009).

This crisis marks, in fact, the end of the possibility of continuing to compensate the internal saving of the countries in surplus with the internal indebtedness of the countries in deficit. "Two years ago," wrote Paul Krugman, "we lived in a world in which China could save much more than it invested and dispose of the excess savings in America. That world is gone." ("China's Dollar Trap," *New York Times*, April 3, 2009). If one indeed wanted to reform the international monetary system in order to avoid reproducing the fundamental imbalances on a global scale, it would be necessary to go in the direction of the institution of a real supranational currency, a pure vehicle of national purchase powers, like the Bancor unsuccessfully proposed by Keynes to Bretton Woods in 1944 or like the supranational currency for years theorized by the French economist Bernard Schmitt.

In this perspective, what is at stake are the possibilities or impossibilities of overcoming the ongoing crisis *politically*, rather than economically. The block of capitalist accumulation on a global scale is interpreted in the light of these contradictory forces, with, on the one hand, the possibility that this crisis will last a very long time or at least will be systematically followed by similar crises, and, on the other hand, the possibility that, in order to overcome the crisis, the international monetary system will be redefined in the name of national sovereignty and/or regional poles and the symmetry of commercial exchanges (Martin Wolf, "Why President Obama Must Mend a Sick World Economy," *Financial Times*, January 21, 2009).

In the meantime, we would do well to watch how much of the New Deal the Obama administration will be able to realize. Investments in health, with the reform of health insurance, and investments in education, represent by far the two actions that generate major growth of employment, much more than tax cuts. Yet, today there are no transmission channels of the most available income to the demand of consumer goods (Michael Mandel, "The Two Best Cures For the Economy," *Business Week*, March 23–30, 2009). Among the different actions of the economic revival plan (*Financial Stability Plan* or FSP), there is one in particular that immediately merits being kept an eye on. It is a question of the *Homeowner Affordability & Stability Plan*: on the one hand, such an action wants to revive the demand of housing by lowering mortgage rates and making conventional loans more accessible by injections of liquidity to Fannie Mae and Freddie Mac. On the other hand, it authorizes bankruptcy judges to modify the loans taken by owners of insolvent houses. This action constitutes a precedent of historical import, since, in the US, the loans for primary residences are currently the only ones that cannot be modified in bankruptcy courts (James C. Cooper, "Job One: Build a Flour Under Housing," *Business Week*, March 9, 2009).

As a whole, it is a question of an innovative financial action with regard to all the other interventions to rescue the banking and insurance system provided by the FSP—interventions that so far proved to be decisively ineffective, or were veritable fiascos, in Paul Krugman's words. The provision of mortgage refinance funds for American families is, in fact, the only technical action that will restore value to the derivative assets that are today clogging up the world banking system. Such an intervention would be without immediate effects on the public deficit, as the financing is spread over 30 years of loan contracts. In other words, the plan anticipates saving about 4 million families from foreclosure on their houses, but in such a way that a concrete value of the derivative securitized assets is re-established. The same plan allows the saving of many more banks than the rescue interventions undertaken so far. The principle is clear: *begin from the base in order to reform the monetary system.*

In fact, apart from the technical aspect and the all-American specificity of the intervention measure to help homeowners fallen into the trap of easy loans, what counts in this measure is the principle, the *philosophy* that is at its basis. The latter lends itself to many considerations. In the first place, this action raises, at least incipiently, the question of the *right to social ownership* of a common good, a right that in all evidence is imposing itself on the right to private ownership as the only right conceivable today. In other words, if up until today, the access to a common good had taken the form of *private debt*, from now on it is legitimate to conceive (and reclaim it) the same right in the form of *social rent*. In financial capitalism, social rent assumes the form of redistribution, the way in which society gives everyone the right to live with dignity. As such, social rent is articulable on many terrains, particularly on that of education and access to knowledge in the form of the right to an income of guaranteed study.

In the second place, this New Deal action of the new American democratic administration seems to be able to conjoin two levels, two plans that usually conflict with each other. On the one hand, it is a question of a *local* intervention, with help oriented to a determined level of demand aggregated by intervening precisely where the crisis destroys incomes, job positions, and existences. On the other hand, this action has a *global* dimension to the extent that it aims at restoring economic value to financial instruments that, by definition, are created to be immersed in the global financial circulation, i.e., in portfolios of institutions and investment funds of every kind. One of the worst risks of this crisis is, in fact, the closure of these very nation-states, the race to competitive devaluations in order to regain bits of market by taking them away from others with protectionist actions. This is usually how wars break out.

Finally, this action has the absolutely crucial dimension of *time*, the fact being that the help to families in the form of the guarantee to a social rent is a veritable investment in the future. As we said, the interventions from the base not only allow one to avoid instantaneous and massive increases in the public debt, but these interventions are carried out on a *long* temporal horizon, a horizon within which the qualitative development of the new generation can be better ensured with investments in early childhood, in school, and in the early entrance in the job market.

Taking time means giving each other the means of inventing one's own future, freeing it from the anxiety of immediate profit. It means caring for oneself and the environment in which one lives, it means growing up in a socially responsible way. To overcome this crisis without questioning the meaning of consumption, production, and investment is to reproduce the preconditions of financial capitalism, the violence of its ups and downs, the philosophy according to which "time is everything, the man is nothing." For man to be everything, we need to adapt ourselves to the time of his existence.

Appendix

WORDS IN CRISIS[*]

Finance has its own language and, moreover, a rather esoteric neolanguage. Many Anglo-Saxon terms are untranslatable into other languages and, above all, designate complex processes not always accessible to the uninitiated, which is to say, to almost everyone. It is thus under the shelter of this linguistic opacity that finance prospers, which raises the question of democracy, that is, the possibility of publicly debating strategies, procedures, and decisions concerning the lives of all citizens. In what follows, we have selected some (not all!) words that help readers to understand the history of the most recent financialization.

---

* This brief dictionary was written on the basis of the following publications: *La grande crisi. Domande e risposte*, Il Sole 24 Ore, Milano, October 2008; Charles R. Morris, *Crack. Come siamo arrivati al collasso del mercato e cosa ci riserva il futuro*, Elliot Edizioni, Rome, 2008; Frédéric Lordon, *Jusqu'à quand? Pour en finir avec les crises financières*, Editions Raisons d'agir, Paris, 2008; Paul Krugman, *Il ritorno dell'economia della depressione e la crisi del 2008*, Garzanti, Milan, 2008.

AAA, AA, A, BBB, etc: a system (used by the rating agency Standard & Poor's) of evaluating the quality of debt assets. The more the asset is at risk, the lower is the vote and the higher the earning.

ABCP (Asset-Backed Commercial Paper): a kind of unsecured promissory note (or commercial paper) guaranteed by other financial activities, particularly by securitized assets. The ABCP are generally short-term investments that are due between 80 and 180 days, issued by banks or other financial institutions in order to satisfy the need for short-term financing. These are amply employed in special purpose vehicles sponsored by the banks (see Conduit and SPV) that financed with short-term commercial paper so as to invest in long-term assets representative of the credit that was the guarantee of the ABCP. In 2007 and 2008, the value of these assets has collapsed, which is to say, created a lot of problems for the financial institutions involved, which, no longer being able to finance with commercial paper, had to resort to the line of credit of the sponsoring banks (that provoked a strong increase in interbank interest rates, a clear sign of banks distrusting each other).

ABS (Asset-Backed Securities): loans supplied by banks backed by income from an activity that lies immobile until maturity. But if the bank does not want to wait, it can take this activity, "wrap it up" in obligations bearing interest—"obligations guaranteed by activity"—and sell it to private funds. In such a way, the lent out capital immediately returns and the bank can expand its own activity. The types of loans that are mostly given out with the issuance of ABS are real estate loans, credit for purchasing cars, insurance policies, and credit related to the use of credit cards. In sum, the ABS is an instrument of transferring credit, and the related risks, from the banking balances to third-party non-banking buyers.

ALT-A: a class of loans whose risk profile falls between so-called "prime loans" and "subprime loans." Those who sanction this type of loans usually have a personal history of insolvency, and has a low capacity to produce incomes and so agree to deal with a loan service with a pronounced relationship between the value of loan and income.

Bailout: saving a subject close to bankruptcy by an injection of liquidity.

Basis point: a unit equal to 1/100th of a percentage point, indicating variations in interest rates, exchanges, earnings from T-bills and bonds.

Benchmark: an "objective" parameter of reference, constructed through representative signs of the risk/earning profile of the markets. It is an indication that expresses the risks related to the product of investment sanctioned by a saver and is useful for evaluating the efficiency of the product of investment.

Carry trade: this instrument allows one to take out a money loan in countries that apply low interest rates, especially, but not only, in Japan, and to lend them in countries that apply high interest rates, such as Brazil or Russia.

CDO (Collateralized Debt Obligation): the CDO is a specific category of ABS and assets of fixed income that are not subject to regulation on the markets. Typically, the issuance of CDO starts from a "special purpose vehicle" (SVP, see securitization) that is conferred a complex portfolio of mortgage loans, residential or not, but also corporate obligations of high earning, and more still. The portfolio includes credit of various risks. The CDO is then divided into tranches or classes. The lower and the riskier one (equity tranche) absorbs the first X% of subsequent losses; the tranche (senior tranche) suffers losses only if the total losses of the portfolio exceed the quota absorbed by the lesser ones. By virtue of this protection, the senior tranche usually obtains the maximum rating (valuation), i.e., the triple A. The rating gradually decreases for the lesser tranches. The higher the rating of a tranche, the less is its earning. CDOs are very complex instruments of difficult valuations and are thus rather opaque. They are not homogeneous and, both at the time of issuance and successively, are traded over the counter.

CDS (Credit Default Swap): instruments of a larger family of credit derivatives that agrees to transfer the risk of credit relative to a determined financial activity from a subject intending to purchase a guarantee against risk to a subject intending to lend it. The Credit Default Swap is similar to an insurance policy. The CDS are traded over the counter, i.e., on the parallel markets where contracts and modalities of buying and selling are not standardized and not tied to a series of norms (admission, control, informative obligations, etc) governing official markets.

Collateral: an asset pledged by an agent who owns a debt.

Conduit: the conduit is also known as special purpose vehicle. It has to do with a corporate entity created for a specific purpose, usually by a financial institution. For instance, if a bank wants to securitize a series of real estate loans, it confers these loans on a "special purpose vehicle" created on purpose and, on this basis of activity, the new company issues securitized assets. It is essential that these conduits be not formally tied to the parent company; otherwise, they would be recognized as an integral part of the group and their balances would have to be consolidated, thus impeding the transfer of the risk and the dispersal of requirements of capital. This separation decreases at the moment when (like in 2007–08–09) the bank is in liquidity crisis and is dependent on a sponsoring bank to receive credit.

Credit crunch: a contraction (restriction) of credit supply from the banks following a financial crisis in which they are particularly implicated. It is used to "cool down" the inflation. The constraint of credit thus occurs on the wave of bank failures.

Deleveraging: when investors, who entrusted themselves to high-risk financial instruments—managed by institutions of the so-called shadow banking system—withdraw or threaten to withdraw their money from the markets, the system becomes susceptible to a cycle that is auto-reinforced by a forced liquidation of assets (deleveraging), a process that further increases unpredictability and reduces the prices in an entire series of asset categories.

Derivatives: financial contracts stipulated between two contractors whose value depends on the trend in the underlying activity. Underlying activities can have financial (shares, obligations, interest and exchange rates, stock market indexes) or real nature (as raw materials).

Fair value: literally estimate, fair price; the term was introduced by the accounting principles IFRS (International Financial Reporting Standard). It is a method of valuation based on the presupposition that values in balance reflect "real" values. At times, however, a fair value valuation becomes difficult for some activities, particularly the immaterial activities and some financial activities lacking exchange market.

Hedge fund: these are non-regulated funds that operate in accordance with "short selling," i.e., selling assets betting on a reduction of the market (operations of norm not allowed to other typologies of funds), or, vice versa, to "go long," i.e., speculating on an increase in assets. The assets of hedge funds can be invested in any type of activity permitted by regulation, thus assuming short-term positions or departing from all prudential norms of containment and the division of risk. The objective of these funds is to attain the highest earning between those granted by the market without any preclusion with regard to both the areas of investment and the type of financial instrument. They make big use of derivatives.

Interbank rate: the interbank market is meant to provide for short-term cash imbalances where those who have excessive funds lend them to those who need them. Each morning 50 main European banks must share the interest rates they intend to use in the debit/credit operations with the other banks (inter-bank rate). During the crisis of trust between the banks that broke out with the discovery of the abyss of toxic assets, the interbank rate increased considerably.

LBO (Leveraged Buyout): an operation of acquiring a company with the use of a high financial leverage. The debt owned by the (acquiring) company X, generally obtained by granting concessions on guaranteed shares or property of the (acquired) company Y, is then generally repaid either with cash flows generated by the acquired company or by selling branches of the acquired company (so-called non-strategic business unit).

Leverage: the faculty of controlling a high amount of financial resources through the possession of a small part of such resources, and thus with a low use of capital. For the banks, having caused leverage meant issuing derivative financial instruments with ever-more complex structures.

Libor (London Interbank Offered Rate): the rate of interbank market in London. The Euribor is its European equivalent. These two rates serve as reference for all the other interest rates.

Liquidity (cash): liquidity designates the treasury of an agent; the capacity that offers a market to sell its assets "easily," thus the capacity to cease being assets and become cash.

Mark-to-market: an application of the criterion of fair value to accounting: which is to say, of evaluating the activities at the root of market prices rather than historical cost (the cost at which they were purchased). With a view to establishing the "truth of balances" and rendering them transparent, the accounting norms usually call for using "mark-to-market" to evaluate the financial activity and passivity. With respect to the advantages of reliability and transparency, the mark-to-market criterion can aggravate the unpredictability of shares, with pro-cyclical effects, in periods of strong increases or strong drops of prices on financial instruments.

MBS (Mortgage-Backed Securities): a version of ABS obtained by securitization of real estate credit. Monoline: insurers of bonds.

Non-banking financial system: "The structure of the financial system changed fundamentally during the boom, with dramatic growth in the share of assets outside the traditional banking system. This non-bank financial system grew to be very large, particularly in the money and funding markets. In early 2007, asset-backed commercial paper conduits, in structured investment vehicles, in auction-rate preferred securities, tender option bonds and variable rate demand notes, had a combined asset size of roughly $2.2 trillion. [...] The scale of long-term risky and relatively illiquid assets financed by very short-term liabilities made many of the vehicles and institutions in this parallel financial system vulnerable to a classic type of run, but without the protections such as deposit insurance that the banking system has in place to reduce such risks" (Timothy Geithner, United States Secretary of the Treasury, a speech delivered at The Economic Club of New York, June 2008).

Panic: "Sometimes," writes Krugman, "panic is simply panic: an irrational reaction on the part of investors that is not justified by the actual situation." In such cases, those who remain lucid are rewarded for not losing their head. "In economics, however, the kind of panic that—whatever the motive that gives rise to it—autojustifies itself is much more important. The classic example is that of rushing to cash machines: when those in rush try to withdraw all their savings at the same time, the bank must sell its goods at lowest prices, going bankrupt as a consequence; those who do not allow themselves to be seized by panic are worse off than those who effectively lost their head."

Price/earning ratio or P/E: indication given by the relationship between the quotation of a stock price and earning per share. If, for instance, the price/earning ratio of a share equals 15, the stock pays 15 x for generated earnings (example: with a P/E of 15 and a share price of $1, we have an earning rate of 6.7%).

Private equity: investment on the part of specialized subjects in quoted and non-quoted companies. The operator of private equity is a subject financing small companies with good prospects of development, with the intention to make them grow and then demobilize its shareholding at higher prices.

Rating agency: an agency specialized in valuation (notation) of the credit risk of an issuer of obligations, that is, of structured obligations guaranteed by a plurality of mortgage loans. The main agencies are Moody's, Standard & Poor's, Fitch, and DBRS, all American.

Ratio: a relation, indicator resulting from comparison of two quantities, for instance the profit of a company and its assets.

ROE (Return On Equity): the earnings from net assets. It indicates the profitability of their own means, that is, those made available by shareholders of a company (such as a bank).

Securitization: consists of the transformation (giving way to a "special purpose vehicle" or SVP that has as its exclusive objective the realization of such operations) of credit, or also of future cash flows, into an asset. Example: let us suppose that the bank has a number of real estate loans between its activities; the bank can decide to securitize them, i.e., to issue securities that have these loans as the guarantee. These securities are then sold to private or institutional investors and the bank thus returns the money to the lenders: the funds that the bank obtains can be used to expand its own activity. The securitized assets, like normal obligations, have a maturity date and an interest rate, and the debt service is tied to refunds and payments of interest on the part of the original debtors. The bank, besides having the advantage of mobilizing activities of little liquidity, also diminishes the risk tied to those loans: the risk is passed on to the investors. The government, on a state or local level, can securitize as well.

SPV (Special Purpose Vehicle): see Conduit.

Subprime: in American language, subprime are real estate loans of lesser quality offered to subjects with high risk of insolvency: with previous episodes of insolvency, with low or even uncertain incomes, lacking other forms of wealth.

Swap: an agreement between two parties who decide to periodically exchange incoming or outgoing cash flows in accordance with preestablished conditions.

Systemic risk: a situation in which a local failure triggers a series of other failures with the threat of global collapse of the financial system.

Toxic asset: "toxic" financial assets are comprised of irrecoverable credit "contaminating" banking balances and, consequently, creditor companies. The "toxic assets" can also end up in the portfolios of savers. Once they would have been defined as "waste paper" or garbage.

ACKNOWLEDGMENTS

The first version of this text was published in a book edited by Andrea Fumagalli and Sandro Mezzandra, *Crisi dell'economia globale. Mercati finanziari, lotte sociali e nuovi scenari politici* (Ombre Corte/ *Uni*nomade, Verona, 2009). I thank Gianfranco Morosato, director of Ombre Corte, and the coauthors of the volume for having me write and republish, in a rather revised and updated form, this essay. I also thank my colleagues at the social research center with Dipartimento di Scienze Aziendali e Sociali della Scuola Universitaria Professionale della Svizzera Italiana (SUPSI) for having discussed the version that is published here. In particular, I thank the colleagues Spartaco Greppi and Federico Corboud for helping me to deepen a lot of questions related to financialization, offering their competence, their time, and their friendship. A personal acknowledgment goes to Fabio Casagrande, Matteo Terzaghi, and Silvano Toppi for encouraging me to publish this work in a short time.